Prai

MW00655851

"*Nothing But The Truth* is truly a unique primer for all investigators and intelligence officers who need to evaluate the truthfulness of their sources. It is a heavily researched and sourced book about a vital part of intelligence tradecraft—asset validation.

—Jack Devine, author of *Good Hunting: An American Spymaster's Story*, former head of CIA operations outside the United States

"Maryann Karinch has not just produced a field manual to ferreting out lies, but a guide to life itself. In every page of *Nothing But the Truth*, Karinch outlines practical techniques of establishing truth in human relationships. In the last chapter, in a sudden turn, Karinch—gently and cheerfully—challenges the reader to turn these same techniques on themselves. In an armchair world of narcissism, habitual self-deception, and whining justification, Karinch is a horn calling through the mist: clear, unwavering, inspiring us to ride out on the hunt."

— Ethan Gutman, author of *The Slaughter*

SECRETS FROM TOP INTELLIGENCE

EXPERTS TO CONTROL

CONVERSATIONS AND GET THE

INFORMATION YOU NEED

NOTHING BUT THE
TRUTH

MARYANN KARINCH

CAREER
PRESS
Pompton Plains, NJ

NOTHING BUT THE TRUTH
EDITED BY JODI BRANDON
TYPESET BY EILEEN MUNSON
Cover design by Howard Grossman/12E Design
Printed in the U.S.A.

To order this title, please call toll-free 1-800-CAREER-1 (NJ and Canada: 201-848-0310) to order using VISA or MasterCard, or for further information on books from Career Press.

The Career Press, Inc.
220 West Parkway, Unit 12
Pompton Plains, NJ 07444
www.careerpress.com

Library of Congress Cataloging-in-Publication Data
CIP Data Available Upon Request.

Dedication

To those who seek
the truth and share it,
most notably
my mother,
my brother Karl,
and Jim.

»«

Acknowledgments

Almost everyone I know has had a career he or she enjoyed, but I can't think of too many people who feel that their career reflected an abiding passion. Not so with the intelligence professionals I've known. My friends and colleagues who have served us all through their careers in the intelligence field are passionate about getting the truth and "telling truth to power." We also benefit from their willingness to give us tips and tell us stories that help us develop some portion of their skill set. With that in mind, I'd like to thank the following contributors to this book who are, or have been, intelligence professionals (in alphabetical order): Elizabeth Bancroft, Ray Decker, Jack Devine, Peter Earnest, Gary Harter, Gregory Hartley, Oleg Kalugin, Eric Maddox, David Major, James O. Pyle, Michael T. Reilly, and Lena Sisco.

Many other professionals in the fields of mental health, medicine, law, journalism, sports, and business—all of them passionate about their work as well—also contributed critical information and insights to this book, and for those thoughts, I thank the following (in alphabetical order): Wendy Aronsson, Harvey Austin, Brian Boitano, Epic Bill Bradley, Trevor Crow, Jeremy Hobson, Dean Hohl, Ryan Holiday, Jim McCormick, Patti Mengers, Ira Neimark, Sue Rotolo, Deborah Schroeder-Saulnier, and Robert L. Saloschin.

I also drew from some outstanding research, as well as riveting interviews and feature pieces on National Public Radio and other media sources. Although I didn't speak with these people personally, I admire their work and I hope that shows in the context of this book: NPR/Radiolab's Ellen Horne, NBC's Brian Williams, psychologist Paul Ekman, social psychologist Amy Cuddy, NPR/Fresh Air's Terry Gross, and body language expert Janine Driver.

Thanks also to people who helped me in valuable ways such as modeling for a photo, discussing the meaning of truth, introducing me to people in the book, and much more: my mother, Judith Bailey, Mary Ann Saloschin Nichols Hubbard, Neita Saloschin, Karen Pedone, Joan Brandt, Travis Phipps, Kevin Sheridan, Stephanie Danyi, Michael Dobson, Kurtis Kelly, David Kozinski, and Larry Atkins. Also, thanks to my sisters in PEO Chapter IY Estes Park for your unwavering moral support and the occasional glass of wine.

Finally, this book would not be possible without the outstanding Career Press team: Ron Fry, Michael Pye, Adam Schwartz, Kirsten Dalley, Laurie Kelly-Pye, Karen Roy, and Jeff Piasky.

The truth is, if I forgot to mention someone, please know that I appreciate what you did, too!

Contents

As long as I have worked with Maryann Karinch, her overriding interest has been to understand how people communicate and how to tell when they're telling the truth and when they're lying. In pursuit of her driving interest, she has interviewed a wide range of professionals who engage with people for a variety of purposes: law enforcement officials, journalists, intelligence officers, medical doctors, academics, and numerous others.

From her many interviews and extensive research, she has identified some key factors and guidelines you can apply in sharpening your own capabilities for judging the veracity of what others are telling you. She has published several books on in this field, though I consider the present the most comprehensive distillation of her observations and thinking.

Most of my career in the Central Intelligence Agency (CIA)'s Clandestine Service as a case officer was devoted to recruiting and running clandestine sources or agents. Developing close relationships with foreigners, let alone assessing them as potential clandestine sources, is a challenging and often drawn-out process in itself.

The recruitment process is usually overlooked or given short shrift in films and popular thrillers on espionage. In these portrayals, individuals are simply "recruited": no details on how or for what reason are given. The book's sections on rapport building and motivators are particularly applicable for this developmental side of operations.

In fact, recruitment and the secure management of clandestine sources is the essence of most clandestine operations in the HUMINT (human intelligence) field. Creating and sustaining relationships with potential sources, those with access to the intelligence, usually takes time and requires the case officer to simultaneously assess the individual's access to intelligence and his personality; that is, would he consider becoming a clandestine source, and if so, why? What would motivate him?

People's motivations for working secretly with the CIA are varied, as are their personal and professional lives, their sense of secrecy, their personalities, and their ways of expressing themselves. Some report their information only in hushed spoken exchanges; others speak from hastily scribbled notes; others deliver immaculately prepared typed reports; and others pass along copies of highly classified (stolen) documents.

Besides trying to understand agents' reporting (often delivered in a safe house or in a car in the dark of night), the case officer must also continuously assess his own agent: how did he acquire his information, and is he reporting as accurately as possible? These are daunting tasks performed within the framework of the case officer's need to keep the agent motivated and on target. The author's thoughts on "managing the exchange" are right on the mark.

You can understand that many of the factors the author raises and discusses in her book—from rapport building and motivating to questioning and managing the exchange—apply directly to my work with clandestine sources. Indeed, it's hard to find a chapter in her book that doesn't apply in some way to the work of recruiting and managing sources.

While my CIA work was in the arcane field of clandestine operations, anyone who deals regularly with people in the course of his or her working life—and that includes most of us—will find some terrific insights and tips in Maryann's book for use in the day-to-day business of judging whether other folks are leveling with you—or not.

—E. Peter Earnest
Former Senior CIA National Clandestine Service Officer
Executive Director of the International Spy Museum

My cell phone rang one Monday afternoon. The caller introduced himself and asked if I had a moment to talk about one of my clients at the literary agency. I said, "Sure."

"He's a con man," he said.

The caller was an investigative reporter. The client was someone on the verge of being offered a sizable advance by a major publishing house for his "true stories." My cut would have paid the mortgage for quite a few months.

Do you want to know how stupid I felt? Even before I wrote this book, I supposedly knew all kind of tips and secrets about detecting deception.

After verifying what the reporter told me by doing a search on the man's *real* name, which I had not known, I decided to give myself a break. My first instinct is to trust people. And there may be no greater reason why I'm a good person to write this book.

Because my trusting nature makes me an easy mark, I wanted to know *all* the secrets of people who can not only spot lies and liars, but also get them to tell the truth. My search for

people of skill and reputation who could tell me all about getting the truth out of someone was intense. I wanted to know
everything they knew, back it up with stories and research, and
give it to you.

In short, this book is part of an evolution.

It follows several books covering lie detection to which I
contributed, most notably *How to Spot a Liar,* co-authored with
Gregory Hartley, a well-known human behavior expert. With its
roots in those earlier works, this is a *truth detection* book.

The technical skills that allow you to become a human
polygraph and detect lies involve reading body language, ascertaining the way people sort information, using directed questioning, and using psychological levers that interrogators call
"approaches." In detecting the truth, these skills are valuable—
but you're just getting started. Truth detection also uses a system of analysis to see correlations among facts, and it considers
a person's feelings, motivations, and experiences, all of which
color the truth. The point is not just to identify lies and facts,
but to also see links among them to get a more complete picture of a person, place, thing, or event.

For example, when I read Eric Maddox's gripping narrative about the search for Saddam Hussein, *Mission: Black List
#1,* I knew I had to talk to him about my book. Here was an
interrogator who sought truth, not just facts. What I gleaned
from him both in the book and in conversation was that he was
never satisfied just to know someone was a driver or a cook.
He wanted to know why they did those jobs, what they drove
and what they cooked, and so on. He questioned sources and
contemplated answers until he saw patterns emerge. People
around Saddam were driven by loyalty, fear, and/or greed, and
Maddox wouldn't have known their relative importance if he

hadn't kept probing into the kind of details that other interrogators thought were irrelevant to finding the dictator.

To me, the difference between what some of his colleagues did and what he did might be expressed in terms of Christmas bulbs. Many interrogators collected a lot of facts that ended up looking like this (right):

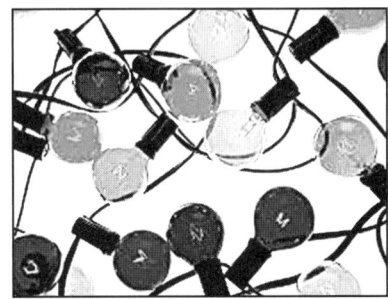

There was no question about it: The facts were important. They were "bright lights." However, the truth was the result of making sense of what they had in front of them (right):

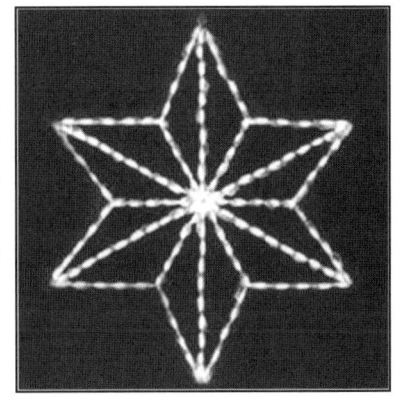

The experts who generously contributed to this book want to help you learn how to get that complete picture. A great deal has to do with the quality of your connection to your source, so many of the insights in the book focus on how to build, and leverage, trust.

Another key skill is analysis. As Peter Earnest, former senior CIA Clandestine Service officer and author of the Foreword for this book, told me, "The ability to turn the words of whatever source into intelligence depends on the person doing the analysis." In the context of your life, you are both the collector of information and the analyst.

Truth may be a hard concept to define, but we all have a sense of it. We probably have a much clearer sense of what deviation from the truth sounds and looks like. The rest of this book offers psychological insights about why the truth is hard to get and how you can get closer to it. It details psychological and emotional levers to get people to cooperate with you. And it relates true stories, examples, and exercises that guide you in applying the ideas discussed.

PART I

Building the Skills

What Do We Mean by "Truth"? 1

Three things cannot be long hidden: the sun, the
moon, and the truth.

—Buddha

The only way you're going to get the truth is if it
comes willingly from the other person.[1]

—Eric Maddox,
the Army interrogator who located Saddam Hussein,
and author of *Mission: Blacklist #1*

Intelligence professionals have a duty to speak truth to power.
In the case of officers in the Central Intelligence Agency
(CIA) in the United States or MI6 in Great Britain "power"
is a head of state whose decisions can affect millions, even billions, of people. Intelligence pros in the corporate environment inform and advise senior executives whose decisions
impact jobs and salaries throughout a company.

People like that had better know what "truth" is before they
start talking to "power." So I asked many intelligence professionals how they define truth. They would usually begin with a
simple phrase you might see in the Oxford Dictionaries—"that

which is in accordance with fact or reality"—but the follow-up invariably addressed the complexity of truth. Based on what they said, in optical terms, I would define truth as white light: It's what we see when all the colors come together.

Truth is rooted in fact, but personal imagination, beliefs, and experiences affect how we process the facts. Emotions and interpretations are therefore parts of the spectrum that compose the truth. If we're missing some of the facts and/ or missing the human responses to them, then the truth has eluded us. Just as the opposite of "fact" may be "lie," the opposite of "truth" could be defined as "inability to see the whole."

Because of our imagination, beliefs, and experiences, human beings are capable of synthesizing ideas and points of view in a way that transcends mere computer-like analysis of data points. We don't just sort the data, organizing them into neat columns; we make sense of them. We connect facts and ideas in uniquely personal ways to arrive at the truth.

An example of this from history has stuck with me many years because is one of the most inspiring tales of problem-solving I've ever heard. The United States Department of Justice under Attorney General Robert Kennedy was in a quandary as to how to stop certain Southern states from allow-ing racial discrimination. Many state and local laws dictated the rules of segregation, in which blacks and whites were to sit on the bus and at bus stations, the use separate rest rooms and separate lunch counters, and so on.

Along came the Freedom Riders, who challenged those practices and wanted to end such segregation. The first Freedom Rides on public buses originated from Washington, D.C. on May 4, 1961. This non-violent protest and those that followed stirred up the anger of white segregationists who turned the Freedom Rides into bloody events at terminals and on buses.

Robert Kennedy wanted an immediate way to sedate the violence, but analyzing the known options didn't point to any quick solution:

▶ It would not be possible to get action from Congress because a large part of the Democratic membership of Congress was made up of Southern Democrats who wouldn't buck the will of their constituents.

▶ Going to court to get an order either to stop the demonstrations or to stop the discriminatory practices—with the latter being preferable—would have taken a year due to appeals, and this was an immediate problem with people getting hurt.

▶ Using the U.S. military was also impracticable for both legal and operational reasons.

Then a Justice Department lawyer named Robert Saloschin remembered something he had read about 10 years earlier. When he had first worked in Washington as a young lawyer, he was with the Civil Aeronautics Board (CAB). Part of his job was to read the laws under which the CAB operated, enacted in 1938. He recalled reading a section pertaining to interstate commerce, which, in very general and sweeping language, prohibited airlines from any form of discrimination, such as carrying cargo for Company A and refusing to carry cargo for Company B. He had a hunch that the language had been copied precisely from earlier laws regulating other modes of interstate transportation (railroads, trucks, and buses). This hunch wasn't an intuitive response, but rather the direct result of allowing his experience and imagination to help him process the facts at hand.

Saloschin told Kennedy that he might find the same provision that was in the CAB law—word for word—when Congress decided to cover interstate buses. It took five minutes to find it.

Saloschin was correct. The language was there—and it could be interpreted to read that *any* kind of discrimination was prohibited by the law. Based on such an interpretation, the Justice Department filed a petition *that day* with the Interstate Commerce Commission (ICC) under that section of the law relating to interstate buses to order the bus lines to stop discrimination in their buses and terminals. The ICC was shocked. Despite their experiences with discrimination that took the form of uneven services to competing companies or financial inequities in the cost of transporting goods, they had never had anything to do with racial inequality before.

The FBI was ordered to go into bus terminals and take pictures of the "white" and "colored" signs in restrooms and waiting rooms. Evidence in hand, on November 1, 1961, the ICC ordered the bus companies to stop the discriminatory practices, and that ended the problem.

Now turn that thought about the way we process information upside down: Sometimes people process input in a way that completely distorts the facts; they wouldn't be able to tell you the truth if their lives depended on it. This is sometimes the case after a traumatic incident in which a victim provides "facts" about when, where, and how an event occurred, and very little matches what actually happened. In those cases, personal experience involves such upsetting emotions that memory can't be relied upon. This phenomenon is at the heart of the work done by The Innocence Project, a national litigation and public policy organization dedicated to exonerating wrongfully convicted individuals.

Eyewitness misidentification is the single greatest cause of wrongful convictions nationwide, playing a role in nearly 75 percent of convictions overturned through DNA testing. Research shows that the human mind is not like a tape recorder; we neither record events exactly as we see them, nor recall them like a tape that has been rewound.[2]

Based on these observations, I would assert that telling the truth and distorting the truth are both human abilities. The day a computer tells you the truth is the day it should be able to vote, get health insurance, and write great novels. Because truth-telling is a human ability, to get to the truth from another person, you sometimes need well-honed interpersonal skills. In the words of Eric Maddox, whose quote helped open this chapter, "The only way you're going to get the truth is if it comes willingly from the other person." Polygraph machines don't have interpersonal skills. A polygraph is not about truth; it is about perception of fact.

You can differentiate between lies and facts through techniques covered in this book, but you must build on those skills to discover the truth. Many secrets of top intelligence experts center on identifying a reliable source and how to build a trusting relationship with that person. They also cover how to dig into the mind of the source to spot biases and motivations. Finally, they focus on analyzing the content at hand to arrive at a multifaceted, multidimensional picture of people, places, things, and events in time.

Their techniques are fundamental to becoming skilled at truth detection. They are useful whether you need the truth from someone in an interview, a negotiation, an investigation, or a discussion about a personal relationship.

Where Do the Facts Come From?

If we have more than five senses—sight, touch, smell, hearing, and taste—then we need an understanding of "fact" that goes beyond what those five animal senses capture.

On August 8, 1920, Austrian philosopher Rudolf Steiner gave a lecture titled "Man's Twelve Senses in Their Relation to Imagination, Inspiration, Intuition." It reflects the evolution of Steiner's thinking that development of these abilities might enable people to explore the spiritual world the way science lets us investigate the physical world. And he thought that the way to develop them was to coordinate the use of the following 12 senses: sight, taste, warmth, hearing, smell, language, touch, balance, thinking, self-movement, ego (understood as a critical element of personality), and life (the perception that we *are*).

Fast-forward to more current conversations about the senses and you may find a lot more than 12 cited. The logic behind the expansion is that each sense is linked to a sensor, and each sensor picks up something unique. For example, sight is actually two senses: the perception of light intensity and the perception of color. If someone invades your house in the middle of the night and all you see is a figure that's roughly 6 feet tall moving through a dark room, you really don't know if that person is white, black, or as green as the Wicked Witch of the West. Your sense of color is not able to function.

From a scientific point of view, Steiner was right about balance because sensors in our ears enable us to detect our orientation; they give us a sense of balance. He was also right about warmth, because there are nerve endings that are dedicated to sensing heat. It's the same with cold, pain, itch, and pressure.

Steiner was also in sync with modern science about his designation of self-movement as a distinct sense. In an article on Howstuffworks.com titled "How Many Senses Does a Human Being Have?" the author notes: "In your muscles and joints, there are sensors that tell you where the different parts of your body are and about the motion and tension of the muscles. These senses let us, for example, touch our index fingers together with our eyes shut."[3]

In giving complete facts about climbing the Matterhorn—that is, facts that take *all* applicable senses into consideration—you would therefore include a description of how your body felt as it moved vertically in addition to what Zermatt, Switzerland, looks like from the summit.

In short, if you think about all the things your body tells you in a given day, you can probably come up with 20 or more distinct senses, including a sense of when you have to urinate and when you've had too much to eat. And among those, we haven't even mentioned the proverbial "sixth sense," meaning an intuitive faculty that can't be easily explained by referring to the sensors in our body.

So where do the facts come from? All of these sources of data collection we call senses.

In *Blink*, Malcolm Gladwell adds another dimension to our thinking about what constitutes a perceived reality. He opens the book with a riveting story about the J. Paul Getty Museum's acquisition of a statue believed to be created about 530 BC. For 14 months, a scientific team analyzed the statue with tools of modern science and declared it authentic. The Museum publicized its extraordinary purchase with the *New York Times* running a front-page feature in fall 1986 on this rare piece ancient art—only to question the authenticity of the purchase five years later.[4]

In the meantime, what had happened wasn't so scientific—that is, explicitly analytical. Shortly after fall 1983, when the statue first came to the Museum, various art historians and other art experts had their first glance at the statue. Their reactions could best be categorized as somewhere between disbelieving and critical about the authenticity of the piece.[5] They didn't use electron microscopes, mass spectrometry, X-ray diffraction, and X-ray fluorescence to reach their conclusions, as the Getty's science experts were doing; they eyeballed the piece. In this summary, Gladwell refers to four world-renowned art experts who immediately identified the statue as a fake:

> When Federico Zeri and Evelyn Harrison and Thomas Hoving and Georgios Dontas—and all the others— looked at the kouros and felt an "intuitive repulsion"— they were absolutely right. In the first two seconds of looking—in a single glance—they were able to understand more about the essence of the statue than the team at the Getty was able to understand after fourteen months.[6]

Combining the rapid gut response described by Gladwell—a kind of instantaneous processing of a multisensory experience—with the slower processing of the Getty Museum's science team, you can arrive at an awareness of how much information may go into a single fact, such as whether or not a statue is authentic.

How Do Imagination, Beliefs, and Experiences Shape the Facts?

What we perceive as truth brings at least three interrelated elements into play: imagination, belief, and experience.

Truth and Imagination

Imagination is a precious gift, enabling us to explore the what-ifs of life. As individuals we are on a continuum in terms of how imagination- and logic-based we are.

Some psychiatrists use a simple test designed by the father-son team of Herbert and David Spiegel to make the determination of a where a person lies on that continuum. Now deceased, Herbert Spiegel was clinical professor of psychiatry at Columbia University and probably best known for his treatment of the woman with multiple personalities called Sybil. David Spiegel is associate chair of psychiatry at Stanford University. Both achieved status as world-renowned experts in the clinical uses of hypnosis. It is their focus on hypnosis that led them to develop the test to determine how trance-prone a person is—that is, how easily someone daydreams and can let imagination take hold, putting logic and reality aside for a while. The test helps the clinician evaluate a person's space awareness, time perception, myth-belief premises, and processing style.[7] It poses questions such as "When you're in a theater watching a play or movie, do you ever get so into it that it takes you a few moments to get reoriented after the curtain comes down?"

This capacity has relevance in a discussion of truth because the ability to allow the mind to wander into what-ifs is one of the ways to understand why a great many people buy into conspiracy theories. And if you have any doubt that this is a lot of people, consider the study "Conspiracy Theories and the

Paranoid Style(s) of Mass Opinion," published in the March
2014 *American Journal of Political Science*. University of
Chicago researchers J. Eric Oliver and Thomas J. Wood took
an unprecedented look at the nature of mass public support
for conspiracy theories. They concluded: "Using four nation-
ally representative surveys, sampled between 2006 and 2011,
we find that half of the American public consistently endorses
at least one conspiracy theory.... In contrast with many the-
oretical speculations, we do not find conspiracism to be a
product of greater authoritarianism, ignorance, or political
conservatism."[8]

They determined that people very likely support conspiracy theories because of a willingness to believe in forces that
are unseen yet intentional, and who feel drawn to narratives
about the struggle between good and evil. In other words,
they are talking about people whom the Spiegels might label
"trance-prone," having the ability to dissociate in a way that
gives rise to imagination.

In commenting on the study for National Public Radio,
NPR's social science correspondent Shankar Vedantam added
another insight to the explanation of why Americans—perhaps,
especially Americans—are so prone to believe in conspiracy
theories:

> [T]he stereotype about people who believe such theo-
> ries is that they're poorly educated, or superstitious or
> that they are political partisans. It turns out the con-
> sistent predictor of such beliefs is something that you
> might almost call an all-American attitude—a belief
> in individualism, distrust of authority. And together
> those things translate into a desire to avoid being con-
> trolled by large secret forces.[9]

Former FBI Supervisory Special Agent David Major, the first director of Counterintelligence, Intelligence and Security Programs on the National Security Council Staff at the White House, approaches the reason from a complementary angle: "People like to believe in conspiracies because it's the nefarious 'they' who are responsible for something shocking. We don't know who 'they' are, but if we did know who 'they' are, it would solve a lot of problems."[10]

With these thoughts in mind, we can get a deeper understanding of why people believe conspiracy theories, but that even if a majority of people believe such a theory, that doesn't raise it to the status of truth. Having the awareness and skill to question a conspiracy theory are vital to anyone who wants nothing but the truth.

One of the most enduring conspiracy theories in American history concerns the assassination of President John F. Kennedy. The Gallup organization conducted a poll just before the 50th anniversary of the assassination and found that 61 percent of Americans believe that others besides Lee Harvey Oswald were involved. This is actually down from a high of 81 percent, which Gallup reported in both the mid-1970s and early 2000s.[11]

To explain—at least partially—how we got to this point of delusion, it's important to reference the Russian art of disinformation. Over the years, I've interviewed a number of people in the intelligence community, and they agree that Russian intelligence services have a mastery of disinformation as part of their so-called operational games. This aptitude for getting people to accept false information as true did not diminish with the collapse of the Soviet Union in 1991; it is a distinguishing feature of the KGB's successor, the FSB.

And what do the Russians have to do with the popular theory that the Kennedy assassination was the result of a right-wing conspiracy involving the CIA? They started it. At the time of Kennedy's assassination, retired Major General Oleg Kalugin of the KGB was in New York, conducting espionage and influence operations as a Radio Moscow correspondent with the United Nations. He notes: "We received a cable from Moscow, which bluntly said that we should say that right-wing guys hated Kennedy and they killed him—that it was an American plot to assassinate him.... It was all about blaming Americans—CIA and FBI. 'They are all behind it' was the Soviet line."[12]

The first book asserting the theory was *Oswald: Assassin or Fall Guy?*, written by Joachim Joesten and first published by a British company. Both Joesten and Victor Perlo, the man who reviewed the book for the *New York Times*—thus giving it immense credibility—were instruments of the KGB.[13] Thomas Boghardt, former historian of the International Spy Museum, puts the successful effort into the larger context of Soviet and Russian disinformation activities in modern history in his article "Active Measures," available for download on the Spy Museum website.[14]

Millions of people, therefore, have embraced the conspiracy theory created by the KGB and popularized by people like filmmaker Oliver Stone. They see it as the truth, and no amount of evidence to the contrary is likely to shake them loose of their vision. In fact, as Shankar Vedantam noted in his NPR commentary, people who buy into a conspiracy theory have a tendency to expand the scope of the conspiracy when confronted by facts that refute it:

A conspiracy theory is where you believe in a theory where no matter how much disconfirming evidence comes in, you somehow convert that disconfirming evidence into part of the conspiracy. So with Barack Obama's birth certificate, for example, the moment the birth certificate came out from Hawaii, the people who believe that Barack Obama was not born in the United States would say the Hawaiian hospital now is in on the conspiracy as well.[15]

Truth and Belief

As you consider this passage from Genesis 3:1–7 (*New American Standard Bible*), ask yourself to what extent it rings true for you:

Now the serpent was more crafty than any beast of the field which the Lord God had made. And he said to the woman, "Indeed, has God said, 'You shall not eat from [a]ny tree of the garden'?" The woman said to the serpent, "From the fruit of the trees of the garden we may eat; but from the fruit of the tree which is in the middle of the garden, God has said, 'You shall not eat from it or touch it, or you will die.'" The serpent said to the woman, "You surely will not die! For God knows that in the day you eat from it your eyes will be opened, and you will be like God, knowing good and evil." When the woman saw that the tree was good for food, and that it was a delight to the eyes, and that the tree was desirable to make one wise, she took from its fruit and ate; and she gave also to her husband with her, and he ate. Then the eyes of both of them were opened, and they knew that they were naked; and they sewed fig leaves together and made themselves loin coverings.

If you take the Bible literally, you believe it's a fact that a snake spoke to a naked woman and convinced her to do something bad. To you, that's truth. If you take this passage figuratively, you believe that human beings tend to be weak in the face of temptation, so we'd better evaluate our options carefully or we have a lot to lose. The person who takes the passage literally would probably agree with the person looking at it figuratively; they could agree on the truth as it captures the frailty of human will. They would not, however, agree that there is truth in the statement "a snake spoke to a naked woman."

I don't know for sure that a serpent has never spoken, although logic tells me that it's unlikely. Herein lies the crux of the discussion about whether or not certain religious beliefs should be labeled "truth" if the acid test for truth is whether or not it reflects reality.

The difference between the two people and their perception of truth is not a simple matter of logic. That is, it cannot simply be explained by saying that either snakes talk or they don't talk. Although it seems to be true that analytic thinking can temporarily decrease religious belief, even in devout believers,[16] a study done by University of California, Los Angeles (UCLA), researchers indicates that believers and non-believers actually have a lot in common in terms of their perception of what's true and what isn't. The study, conducted by Sam Harris, Jonas Kaplan, and colleagues, was the first to compare religious faith to ordinary belief at the level of the brain.[17]

Until the early part of the 20th century, we had little hard evidence to go on—that is, brain science—to determine whether or not religious believers and non-believers differ in how they evaluate what is factual. With the advent of functional magnetic resonance imaging (fMRI), we can now view images of the brain in action, and see how the brain responds when it's in a state of belief or disbelief. In fact, there is a place where "faith happens" in the brain, whether it reflects a belief that Jesus Christ is the son of God or that Eric Clapton is the best rock guitarist who's ever lived. Another way to describe what happens in the brain is to say that our capacity to believe isn't content-driven in that sense that a religious belief doesn't show up in a brain scan as any different from a political or a cultural one.

Bottom line: Our magical brains decide what's true regardless of content. It doesn't really matter if you're religious or non-religious. The biology of the human brain gives us essentially the same capacity to embrace something as truth because, for whatever reason, we happen to believe it is. A person who is convinced the person in the adjacent apartment is from another planet would therefore pass a polygraph when asked if his neighbor is an extraterrestrial.

Sam Harris asserts that this finding may someday give us tools to determine "belief detection" in a manner analogous to how we now to do "lie detection." It's another layer of analysis in determining whether you are hearing nothing but the truth.

Truth and Experience

Wendy Aronsson is a psychotherapist who has been counseling individuals, couples, and families for more than 25 years. She has heard "true stories" that don't quite fit with what she knows to be factual about the person's situation or feelings. And yet, in order to help people, she needs to respect that the stories are their truths. Aronsson, author of *Refeathering the Empty Nest,* wouldn't be able to build the trust necessary to have productive, healing sessions with them if she nit-picked a story about painful moments with a spouse. It's the pain of the relationship that demands her focus, with the details of the story having relevance, but perhaps not dominance.

Aronsson explains, "Two people can be looking at the same thing and describe it quite differently. Their truths are not identical because of the experiences they bring to the table."[18] Though this appreciation for individual perspective may not play well with law enforcement, for example, it is essential and valid for professionals like Aronsson.

That said, omissions or distortions of salient facts undermine her ability to help. So there's a balancing act in any session: The extent to which a therapist takes what the client says as "truth" is affected by the extent to which knowing the facts is the only way the therapist can really help the person.

Trevor Crow, also a therapist, offers a wonderful example of how experience shapes truth in a book we wrote together: *Forging Healthy Connections*. It's the story of Diane and Mike, and how their perspectives on her friends nearly tore them apart. Diane genuinely saw some women who had done exploitive, and even abusive, things to her as friends; in contrast, Mike saw them as people who had a keen sense of how to victimize both him and Diane. Each held fast to what she and he perceived as the truth.

Diane's "truth" disintegrated when Trevor told the couple the story of scorpion and the frog, and then explored why Diane was a frog. The story goes like this: The scorpion is catching a ride across the river by riding on the back of the frog. He stings the frog on the head. As the frog is dying, he whimpers, "Why did you do that to me?" The scorpion replies, "I'm a scorpion, dummy."[19]

What Diane rapidly realized was that her bullying older sister, who had the mother's relentless affection, had gotten her accustomed to associating "accepting the status quo" with "keeping the peace." As soon as Mike understood Diane's "truth," he could move closer to her. The happy ending is that they came together to see her exploitive friends and their antics the same way. Their shared experiences altered what both of them would now consider the truth.

More common examples of how personal experience affects the way a person processes facts concern dating, eating, driving, and other day-to-day events. Your hostess asks, "Why won't you eat your lamb chop?" You answer that you've never had a lamb chop you've liked. So is the truth of that exchange that lamb chops taste bad? No. The fact is, you've never eaten a lamb chop you liked, but the truth is, you might like one that was prepared well.

So What Is Truth?

Truth embodies facts collected as a result of sensory input, but it also captures relationships between and among pieces of information.

Two facts may be that Mark works in New Orleans and flies home to Philadelphia on weekends. If you knew nothing else, as is the case with many of his coworkers, you might draw the conclusion that he hates New Orleans and misses Philadelphia. The truth is that he loves New Orleans, but his wife won't move there with the children because her social circle is in Philadelphia. So every weekend, he leaves the place he would like to call home and goes back to a city he's never enjoyed. In this story, a fundamental element of the truth is the person's feelings.

Truth has a foundation in reality. A person's imagination, beliefs, or experiences have the power either to illuminate that reality or to make it hard to see.

Integrity is telling myself the truth. And honesty is
telling the truth to other people.

> —Spencer Johnson,
> author of *Who Moved My Cheese?*

News often provokes the question "Who's telling the truth?"
During development of this book, three people surfaced in
the news daily and all of them had millions of people asking,
"Can we believe him?" It was an important question because
each newsmaker's actions affected people in many places
around the world.

Some people asked a deeper question related to their
statements: "Does he believe himself?" That is, does the person himself think he is telling the truth?

The three people are Edward Snowden, Barack Obama,
and Vladimir Putin, and it's their widespread influence
through word and deed that was the basis for my decision to
discuss them here. We are all in a position to vet the source
when it comes to such prominent individuals. We can accomplish it through a combination of critical thinking and techniques the intelligence pros use to read people.

The central fact is undisputed when it comes to Edward Snowden: He leaked classified documents describing surveillance activities of the National Security Agency to media. Those documents covered both domestic and international activities, and therefore affected perceptions around the world of how the United States collects intelligence. (In this context, I define intelligence as something of political, geopolitical, or military value.)

In contrast to the undisputed fact of what Snowden did, the truth of what he did, as well as what followed, is disputed. Key issues include whether or not he ever tried to alert anyone in Congress or the government about his concerns, whether or not he took steps to ensure that no one would be harmed by the leaks, and the reason he ended up in Russia. Controversy over such issues has given rise to conflicting headlines:

"Edward Snowden: Whistleblower or Traitor?"
(*Al Jazeera*, June 8, 2014)

"Edward Snowden's NSA Leaks 'An Important Service,' Says Al Gore" (*The Guardian*, June 10, 2014)

"More Americans Oppose Edward Snowden's Actions Than Support Them" (NBC News, June 1, 2014)

"House Members to Edward Snowden: No Mercy" (Politico, May 22, 2014)

"Snowden Leaks Have Hurt American Companies, Tech Executive Says" (*Time*, June 9, 2014)

A little foreshadowing of a discussion in Chapter 8 on the value of yes-or-no questions with a source who has something to hide gives insights as to why it is so easy for the media and the public to adopt radically opposing views of the truth in this case. In the interview conducted by Brian Williams for NBC News,[1] Snowden handled some critical yes-or-no questions as follows:

Williams: "To your knowledge, there is nothing you have turned over to the journalists that is materially damaging or threatening to the national security?"

Snowden: "There is nothing that would be published that would harm the public interest."

Williams said in his commentary immediately following that portion of that interview, "Note that Snowden didn't deny turning over military secrets." In saying that, Williams highlighted the fact that Snowden didn't answer the question with a simple no. Therefore it's possible that he gave the media documents that could hurt national security.

Later, Williams asked him, "In your mind, are you blameless? Have you done, as you look at this, just a good thing? Have you performed, as you see it, a public service?"

Snowden: "I think it can be both."

This is a curious answer to another yes-or-no question, as it's not clear what "both" refers to. Further, Snowden follows it with what appears to be a planned response about the difference between what is right and what is legal—a setup for a discussion of the value to democracy of civil disobedience. In my past life as a marketing communications executive who sometimes coached my bosses prior to media interviews, I would teach this as a tactic to stay on point. That is, the interviewee walks into the interview knowing that certain points must be made in order to get the complete message across in the interview. Therefore, any question that even brushes up against the topic is an opening to deliver that part of the message.

In the case of Edward Snowden, the listener's/viewer's point of view makes all the difference in terms of what is labeled "the truth." To one person, even violation of the U.S. Espionage Act is moral if the public good is somehow served. To another, violating that law and negative effects related to that criminal act mitigate any public good that may have come from the leaks. To the former, the truth is that Snowden is a patriot; to the latter, it is that Edward Snowden is a traitor to the United States.

But the deeper question of "Does he himself think he's telling the truth?" is something that can be answered more definitively. It is also at the heart of an exercise in learning how to vet a source. Later in this chapter is a discussion of both verbal and non-verbal indicators of deception; I return to the Snowden interview by Brian Williams during that discussion.

Turning to President Barack Obama, we first should admit that probably every U.S. president in modern times (meaning we have video and transcripts that enable meticulous fact-checking) has been guilty of misleading or even blatantly false statements. The question is this: Is he speaking what he believes to be the truth, or is he deliberately using language that will disguise the truth in the interests of political gain (or political survival)?

This is one time when advocacy journalists can help us vet the source. These are journalists who openly espouse a point of view and deliver news analysis with that bias made clear. But advocacy journalism can play a role in both undermining the truth and illuminating it. Sometimes, a strident point of view twists facts and integrates warped statistics. Other times, advocacy journalists actually catch a piece of the picture (for example, impact of a new law or regulation on certain populations) that so-called objective journalists completely miss or choose to ignore. For a thoughtful listener or viewer, they provoke questions that enable a person to vet the source.

A good example of confusion about the truth of a U.S. president's statement surfaces in Obama's keynote at the Democratic National Convention on September 6, 2012. Critics of President Obama, as well as those who wanted to believe both the spirit and substance of what he said, locked on to to assertions such as "We've doubled our use of renewable energy, and thousands of Americans have jobs today building wind turbines and long-lasting batteries."
Was the statement factually correct? Did Obama believe it?

The *Washington Post* labeled this statement "true with a (good) but" in its September 7, 2012 article on the speech:

> As [*TIME* magazine's senior national correspondent] Michael Grunwald pointed out on Twitter, this way undersells what happened to green energy under Obama. Wind energy doubled, but solar grew over 600 percent. 85,000 Americans work in wind energy, and in 2010, 5,918 people worked on battery production for electric cars and other renewable energy projects.[2]

In contrast, Politifact.com (produced by the *Tampa Bay Times*) labeled the statement "mostly false." Their definition of "mostly false" is that "The statement contains an element of truth but ignores critical facts that would give a different impression."[3]

Relative to the Obama statement, the facts he did take into consideration are:

▸ Net electricity generation from wind, which more than doubled between 2008 and 2011.

▶ Net electricity generation from solar has more than doubled over the same period.

▶ During the first five months of 2012, the United States has produced more electricity from wind than it did in all of 2008.

These are all verifiable statistics from the Energy Information Administration (EIA), a federal agency that collects energy data.

Politifact.com's determination was that the statement was mostly false. It doesn't say that Obama's presentation of trend information for wind and solar are wrong, but that he used the wrong words to describe the trend for renewable energy as a whole—thus helping to render it inaccurate.

Renewable energy also includes hydroelectric, geothermal, and certain biomass energy. According to Politifact.com:

If you put them all together by BTUs, wind energy in 2011 accounted for 11 percent of all renewable-energy production. That's not 11 percent of all energy production, including coal, oil and natural gas—that's 11 percent of just the production from renewable sources. Solar, meanwhile, was even smaller. It accounted for about 1 percent of all renewable energy production.

If you look at all types of electricity generation from renewables, the increase isn't double between 2008 and 2011—it's 55 percent.[4]

The journalists and researchers at the *Tampa Bay Times* that contribute to Politifact.com went on to point out that "Energy and electricity are not the same thing. Not all renewable energy is used to create electricity." With that as an additional consideration, the impact of renewables slumps lower: "The increase in megawatt hours was about 25 percent, according to EIA data and estimates."[5] But it wasn't Obama who mentioned electricity; it was the spokeswoman from EIA who defended his statement and couched the progress in terms of electricity.

In short, your determination of whether or not Obama thought he told the truth would have to rest on whether or not:

▶ he had reliable advisors about the subject,

▶ he asked good questions about the subject in preparing his speech, and

▶ he comprehended both the science and economics of renewable energy.

In addition, the possibility exists that he deemed the statement "true enough" to use and decided to do so because it would resonate with his audience and the voter base.

The value of this example is suggesting how many variables there are in ascertaining whether a particular person is telling the truth at particular moment in time. And as with the Snowden example, using tools like body language analysis can reveal whether or not the person believes his own words.

Finally, a quick look at Russian President Vladimir Putin gives us more blatant examples of someone who mixes salient omissions and carefully selected facts to project something he wants his audiences to embrace as the truth. Prior to the Sochi Olympics in 2014, Putin's statement about equal rights in Russia sent fact-checkers in many nations scurrying to reliable sources of information about the rights of homosexuals around the world. The controversial Putin statement, made during an interview with ABC's *This Week* (January 19, 2014) and other media outlets, was that in Russia all people are equal, regardless of religion, sex, ethnicity, or sexual orientation, whereas 70 countries in the world have criminal liability for homosexuality.

In a technical sense, Putin was largely correct because homosexuality is not criminalized in Russia, whereas more than 70 countries do have laws on the books banning homosexuality. But his assertion didn't capture the reality of life for homosexuals in Russia, where employers can fire people for being gay, same-sex couples cannot adopt, and lesbians cannot use artificial insemination to bear children.

Putin himself signed a law in June 2013—ostensibly "protecting" minors—that banned "homosexual propaganda." It's broad enough to make events like Gay Pride parades impossible to carry out, presumably because children might be along the parade route. With facts like that in mind, one would have to conclude that Putin deliberately crafted his statement to deceive listeners and readers.

Retired Major General Oleg Kalugin, formerly a top official with the KGB, reinforces that inference by noting: "Nothing is done is Russia today without Putin's consent. He is in charge of everything."[6]

The guidance in this chapter applies to both written and spoken information. The first step is embracing the assumption that what you are about to read or hear cannot be taken as gospel—even if the source is an admired head of state. Keep in mind that even holy leaders such as the Pope and Dalai Lama can make mistakes, too.

Types of Information

There are different types of information, which we might group into the categories of descriptive, anecdotal, statistical, and opinionated: (Examples for the first two kinds of information come with the help of Snopes.com, the excellent Website founded in 1995 by Barbara and David Mikkelson to debunk urban legends and rumors.)

» **Descriptive:** The information depicts and person, place, thing, or event; it might, for example, tell you how to do something. The following pieces of descriptive information are from Snopes.com's medical section:

  ▸ Doctors generally recommend one attempt to cough rhythmically during a heart attack to increase the chance of surviving it. (False)

  ▸ Handles of shopping carts are laden with germs. (True)

» **Anecdotal:** These statements convey a short story about an event or individual. In these examples, the anecdotal information relates to rumors of war in the days after the attacks on September 11, 2001:

  ▸ Three people died of suffocation after sealing their home with plastic sheeting and duct tape. (True)

  ▸ A shipment of UPS uniforms is missing and presumed to have been stolen by terrorists. (False)

» **Statistical:** Statements featuring numerical data fall into this category. Advertisers and politicians are two types of people who often play fast and loose with the numbers:

  ▸ In a January 26, 2014 interview on CNN's *State of the Union*, Senator Rand Paul criticized Obama's job-creation efforts through such programs as loan guarantees and said, "What he [President Obama] misunderstands is that nine out of 10 businesses fail, so nine out of 10 times, he's going to give it to the wrong people."

▶   According to Smallbusinessplanned.com, which
     considered three different studies in determining
     small business survival rates, the reality is that
     the failure rate is 50 percent after four years. The
     rate decreases after that, but the "nine out of 10
     times" statistic is bogus.

»   **Opinionated:** Even information capturing an opinion can
    sometimes get a "false" label because the person who is
    saying it doesn't really hold the opinion:

    ▶   "I think that color looks great on you" is an
         example of opinionated information that might
         have no relationship to the truth for the person
         saying it.

    ▶   An opinionated statement with more global
         significance would be "I believe we have the
         ability to win this war."

Now, let's take a look at the categories with the idea in
mind that you want to vet the source of the information. Key
areas of scrutiny are motivation and presentation.

Motivation

Both types of information can be affected by the motivation of the source. In vetting the source, it is vital to determine
why the person wants to give you the information. Is the person
selling something? Trying to educate? Hoping to impress you?
Wanting to minimize the information exchange? The rapport-
building techniques covered in Chapter 3 help illuminate how
you can ascertain the motivation of a source.

In his book *Good Hunting*, Jack Devine describes the way
the CIA has traditionally recruited and handled agents to get
a clear understanding of their motivation. (An agent in the

context of espionage is someone who provides information or other services covertly to the CIA.) Devine is former deputy director of operations, responsible for all of the CIA's spying operations. He prefaces his remarks by noting that paying for information is actually one way to help clarify the motivation of the source:

> As a general operating principle, we select targets who have known access to information we need. Hence, we start from a very strong position, because the source does not have to invent information to get paid. He or she already has the access. Furthermore, a high percentage of our recruitments begin with ideological identification with the United States. Many of them either don't identify with the political systems in their countries or have been harmed by them. The money is a reinforcing inducement, not the be-all and end-all in a source's productivity. Plus, there is a work ethic among most agents. They respond to financial incentives and try to collect good information to continue earning them. The issue of false or corrupted information comes into play when you have a walk-in (someone who appears at an embassy and volunteers his services) or a double agent.[7]

Presentation

Several types of red flags may go up that should cause you to take a deeper look and remain skeptical. Some of them pertain primarily to descriptive or anecdotal information; others tie in more closely to statistical information. Finally, when it comes to opinionated information, an opinion in and of itself is reason to switch on your internal lie detector; the person's presentation tells you how much to amp it up.

The following two sections provide guidance on verbal and non-verbal aspects, respectively, of a source's presentation that are clues something may be amiss.

Verbal Red Flags
Descriptive or Anecdotal Information

When he was with the FBI managing counterintelligence efforts, David Major's job was to "identify and neutralize individuals spying against America."[8] Major now heads the CI CENTRE, teaching people to identify these red flags in his numerous courses on counterintelligence, including a five-day course on *asset validation*. The asset validation process helps his clients gauge the intentions and veracity of sources and the authenticity of information received from them; in lay-person's terms, we're talking about vetting a source. A couple of the things he tells students to consider are the first two bullet points in the following list; the third and fourth come from James O. Pyle, former U.S. Army interrogation instructor and my co-author of *Find Out Anything From Anyone, Anytime*. The ways to interact with the source when you spot these red flags are described in chapters that follow. But note well: These glitches in communication that signal a problem don't only pertain to a home-grown terrorist who might strap explosives to his body and jump on a D train to Brooklyn. They apply to anyone if your life.

» Look for anomalies in the information. Any gaps or irregularities suggest you need to ask your source more questions. A common example is one that the parent of any teenager can relate to. You say, "We agreed you'd be home by 10. What were you doing that you couldn't get home until 11:30?" Your teenager then gives you a rundown of his evening that doesn't exactly explain the missing 90 minutes.

»   Be skeptical if you don't get a straight answer to a straight question. One of the simplest and most effective tools that any interrogator has is direct questioning. You probably aren't an interrogator *per se*, but when you need to know something about a person, place, thing, or event in time, you often ask a direct question about it. For example, you might ask your spouse why he's worked late four out five nights this week. When his answer dances around that direct question, you have every reason to be suspicious.

»   Be wary if your source majors in the minor information or minors in the major information—that is, if the person seems to be misplacing emphasis that should evoke suspicion about the veracity of the statement. Another way of describing "majoring in minor information" is being hypercritical about some aspect of a statement to distract from a more important discussion. When one of my author friends was accused of a copyright violation because of using a graphic that another author laid claim to, my friend said simply, "I sought permission, you gave it, and I included proper attribution in the book." The aggrieved party, who thought he would make some money if he could prove a violation, came back with an e-mail that accused her not including his Web address in four different locations in the book where he thought it should go. That is, he used nitpicking as a negotiating tactic, putting emphasis on a minor point to distract from the fact that he had no major point.

»   The converse of this is minimizing a significant point. In the copyright example, if my friend had responded to the complainant by casually dismissing the graphic as unimportant to the book's content, noting that readers would pay more attention to a positive story she told about him, she would be minoring in the major information.

» Watch/listen for verb tense changes and pronoun number changes. They are mechanisms people may use, whether consciously or subconsciously, to distance themselves from an event, person, or idea. For example, if a person has been saying, "I did this" and "I went there," and then suddenly switches to "and then we decided to do that," you should wonder who "we" are and why the source felt a need to involve others. There may, in fact, be no "we." It's possible that the change to a plural pronoun is a psychological slip on the part of the source who feels uncomfortable admitting that a particular action was his alone. People often do this to spread the blame for bad decision.

In 1999, rumors started circulating widely that Lance Armstrong was using performance-enhancing drugs. In August 1999, he made his first public statement about the accusation. Oddly enough, at some point, he began talking about himself in the third person: "From the beginning, people didn't want Lance Armstrong for a number of reasons. Either he was not going to be able to race again at a high level or he was a risk of bad publicity."[9]

Similarly, if a person who has been telling you a story in the past tense shifts to a present tense, for example—as though she's putting you into the scene—you have reason to question the presentation. Let's say Sarah's boss has suggested that she's at fault for losing an important client. He asks her what happened at a critical meeting with him. She says: "Zach and I told the client we could have the deliverables by Thursday. We made an appointment to present them at a meeting. So Thursday rolls around and here we are getting ready to walk into the meeting and Zach says to me, 'I wonder how tuned in they are to the importance of social media.'"

Statistical information

As soon as you see or hear statistical information, automatically question it. Jack Devine told me, not jokingly, that when people at the CIA would give him a report with numbers in it, "I would send it back without reading it."[10] His standard request was that whoever submitted the report should go back and check the numbers and flesh out any explanation that would clarify their reliability and value.

Award-winning journalist Glenn Kessler, who contributes to the Fact Checker column for the *Washington Post*, offered these tips on statistics information; these specifically pertain to the failure rate of "9 out of 10 businesses" cited by Rand Paul:

1. What's the time frame? Two years, five years, 10 years? That can make a big difference.

2. Does "fail" mean that it goes out of business because it was not financially viable? Or does that also include data about successful enterprises that merge with another company?

3. Wouldn't failure rates be different for some industries than others? Does it make sense to lump all businesses together?[11]

To make them more generic, consider Kessler's three points in these terms:

▸ Time period covered by the statistics.

▸ Definitions of keywords and concepts.

▸ Similarities and differences between elements of the group covered by the statistics. For example, statistics on "immigrants of color" in the United States would need a clear explanation, because immigrants from the Philippines and Kenya might have very different situations and lumping them together could yield screwed statistical data.

Opinionated Information

At least two types of verbal cues come into play with opinions: the use of modifiers to amplify the point of view, and the use of words that distance the source from the opinion.

Suspect statement with modifiers: "I really believe very strongly that she never would have said that to you if she hadn't been drinking too much."

Less suspect: "I believe she never would have said that to you if she hadn't been drinking."

Suspect statement with distance: "I've always tended to be of the opinion that global warming poses threats to the economy as well as to our health."

Less suspect: "I think global warming poses threats to the economy as well as to our health."

On January 11, 2008, Deepak Chopra posted an essay on the Huffington Post site by author and biologist Rupert Sheldrake, who is most known for his work in parapsychology. In the essay he sent to Chopra, Sheldrake explains how we was suckered into a negative media experience with fellow scientist and well-known atheist Richard Dawkins. It is possible Sheldrake could have prevented the fiasco if he'd had his radar up about the use of modifiers as a warning of deception.

Sheldrake notes that the reluctance he had at first to participate in Dawkins's documentary series was due to a previous television program called *The Root of all Evil*, which was edited to minimize the thinking of everyone except Dawkins. Sheldrake was told the following via e-mail: "...the production team's representative assured me that they were actually interested in facts, and that 'this documentary, at Channel 4's insistence, will be an entirely more balanced affair than *The Root of All Evil* was.' She added, 'We are very keen for it to be a discussion between two scientists, about scientific modes of enquiry.'"[12]

The overcompensating phrases "entirely more balanced" and "very keen" probably stood out to you, and they should. The production assistant's failure to communicate in a straightforward manner about what the program would be—not what it would be in comparison to another show or what the team was "keen" on it being—are signs of an attempt to cloak the truth.

When Sheldrake later challenged the program's director, Russell Barnes, and told him about the assurance the show would be a balanced scientific discussion, Barnes asked for proof. Sheldrake provided the e-mails. He recalls: "He [Barnes] read them with obvious dismay, and said the assurances she had given me were wrong."[13]

David Major provides an additional insight into the kind of statements and behavior—and into the mind itself—of someone who is trying to deceive:

> We taught people in interrogations of criminals to accuse them (allow them to rationalize their criminal activity) of doing the crime. How they respond is very telling about guilt or innocence. The person who is innocent wants to get up and walk out. He's denied the charge and there is nothing more to say. He just gets mad at you. The person who is guilty will hang around; he wants to see what you've got. It's like playing poker. He will stay longer and talk to you. The longer he will stay and talk, the greater the chance he's guilty.[14]

Non-Verbal Red Flags

Lena Sisco offers a course on body-language basics called "How to Be a Body Language Expert: Be a REBLE." Sisco, who is president of The Congruency Group, trains U.S. Department of Defense personnel in interrogation, tactical questioning/debriefing, site exploitation, elicitation, counter-elicitation, cross-cultural communications, human intelligence (HUMINT) policy, detecting deception, and behavioral congruency.

Her term REBLE stands for a five-step program on how to accurately read body language and detect deception: Relax, Establish rapport, Baseline, Look for deviations, and Extract the truth. Chapter 3 is devoted entirely to establishing rapport, and you will do the best job if you are relaxed when you meet the source. For that reason, "R" and "E" will be covered together. Chapters 4 and 5 describe the processes you can use to extract the truth. To complete the discussion of vetting the source, therefore, the focus is on determining baseline and spotting deviations from baseline.

To get a reliable baseline for someone, study that person in an unstressed state. Know how he normally acts as well as sounds. Regarding the latter, if an individual is well-spoken, part of his baseline might be clear and correct pronunciations of words. A deviation from baseline would be suddenly dropping the "-ing" at the end of word and turning into "-in'." I've heard everyone from acquaintances to the president of the United States do this in situations where they are a bit uncomfortable. Yes, this is a verbal red flag, but when you hear it, it's your cue to look for non-verbal signs that reinforce your guess that your source has deviated from baseline.

Some people have quirky movements such as a jumpy foot or an eye twitch even when they're relaxed. These can be part of a person's baseline. So even though you don't see such movements as normal in the context of your own body language, they may be the norm for your source.

There is no absolute rule of where you start in your evaluation of baseline and spotting deviations, so that fact that I'm going from eyes to toes is arbitrary. The organizing principle I'm using is that the eyes are closest to the brain the toes are farthest away.

Eyes

Grasping the meaning of eye movement is considered by many of us to be a foundation skill in lie detection. However, there are at least a couple of schools of thought on how to go about reading eye movement. It should also be noted that psychologists are not in agreement that there is a correlation between eye movement and thought; some actually think it's useless in lie detection. My experience with reading eye movement comes from real-world observation, so I've never conducted tests shaped by rigorous scientific protocols like some of those who debunk the relationship between thought and eye movement. I will say this, though: I've been watching people and doing demonstrations with audience members and body language students for 10 years, and I've seen a great deal of evidence that a correlation exists.

The most popular system of reading eye movement comes out of neuro-linguistic programming (NLP), an approach to performance improvement and communication created by Richard Bandler and John Grinder in the 1970s. The name itself contains the elements that Bandler and Grinder see as connected: "Neuro" relates to nerves or the nervous system; "linguistic" refers to language; "programming" suggests patterns ingrained through experience.

According to NLP, automatic eye movements often correspond to particular thought processes and indicate that a person
is accessing different areas of the brain. Bandler and Grinder
did not originate the idea; they simply took it to a new level. The
idea that eye movements might somehow be related to different
parts of the brain being engaged goes back to William James,
who talked about it in his 1890 book, *Principles of Psychology:*

> In attending to either an idea or a sensation belonging to
> a particular sense-sphere, the movement is the adjust-
> ment of the sense-organ, felt as it occurs. I cannot think
> in visual terms, for example, without feeling a fluctu-
> ating play of pressures, convergences, divergences,
> and accommodations in my eyeballs.... When I try to
> remember or reflect, the movements in question...feel
> like a sort of withdrawal from the outer world. As far as
> I can detect, these feelings are due to an actual rolling
> outwards and upwards of the eyeballs.[15]

In NLP terms, James is describing a "visual eye-accessing
cue"—that is, eyes moving up and to the left or right for visualization. Studies done just before and shortly after Bandler and
Grinder debuted NLP pointed to essentially the same conclusions that they drew about visual and auditory accessing cues
as well as indicators of deep thought or calculation and deep
feelings about someone or something.

Although the left/right relationship might differ from
person to person, the point is that looking to one side signals memory, and other side, imagination, when we're talking
about visual or auditory cues. Eyes down means either emotion or thought.

In this image, the memory and thought cues are to the subject's *right*:

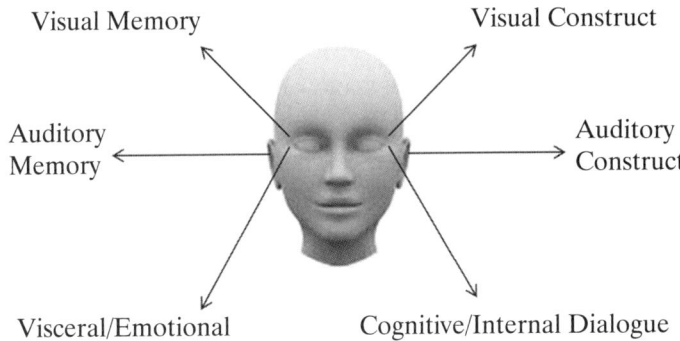

Visual Memory — Visual Construct — Auditory Memory — Auditory Construct — Visceral/Emotional — Cognitive/Internal Dialogue

Following are a few questions you might ask if you want to do casual experiments with people to see how their eyes move in response. Keep in mind that we are about to build on this information with other thoughts on eye movement, so this is not an absolute test:

▶ What does your kitchen look like? (visual memory)

▶ If you could transport yourself to the surface of Venus, what would it look like? (visual construct)

▶ What are the opening notes of your favorite song? (auditory memory)

▶ What do you think a baby giraffe sounds like when she wants her mother? (auditory construct)

▶ How did you feel when you lost someone very close to you—mother, father, friend? (visceral/emotional)

▶ When you bought your last car, what percentage of your income went to payments? (cognitive/internal dialogue)

Although I said earlier that I have seen the NLP system work countless times, I also had it fail me once. In order to help people in the room make sense of what occurred I had to take the focus away from the NLP system and put it on the meaning of what had happened.

In brief, in a Senior Executive Service (SES) class I was teaching for the Department of Homeland Security, students paired up for the eye movement portion of the session. One student asked questions like the previous one, and the other member of the pair responded. The way I do the exercise, no one is briefed in advance on what they might discover; the observer is told simply to observe. With the exception of one pair, I got what I expected, which was affirmation that the way eyes wandered seemed to correlate with thought. Some people were up left for memory, some were up right, and so on. What happened with that lone pair caught me a bit off guard. The observer in the pair described what seemed to her to be random eye movements—nothing that corresponded to what she was now seeing on the NLP chart on the slide I displayed.

It's a prime example of Lena Sisco's caution: "I use NLP, but it's only part of the game. NLP alone is not necessarily accurate. People's eyes move in different directions—lots of different ways."[16]

The question with the SES class was this: Was there a system for reading eye movements like her partner's? The answer: yes, but it sure isn't NLP. The way to read him was to do a thorough baseline before jumping to any conclusions about whether he might be accessing imagination or memory. Watch what his hands do, what his feet do, his facial expressions while he's talking. Listen to his rate of speech, choice of words, and every other aspect of his communication that constitutes what's normal for him. Deviations from that baseline would then be the first signal that perhaps he was constructing information rather than recalling it.

The anomaly was actually a perfect opportunity to reinforce the point that no single system of reading people is 100-percent reliable in giving us a definitive answer on someone's truthfulness. It also proved to be a great setup for the lessons on reading the rest of the body to determine baseline and spot deviations from it.

Face

The ability to manipulate the muscles in the face to convey an emotion should be thought of as being on a continuum. Some emotions are very easy project at will—they are easy to fake—whereas a few others involve facial muscles in such a way that few people have the control needed to fake them. So in an effort to spot deviations from baseline, for now, let's consider facial expressions that are probably unintended.

With the baseline issue in mind, you will not be focused on the universality of certain expressions—that is, the expressions of emotion Paul Ekman identified as common to all humans: disgust, sadness, anger, fear, surprise, and happiness. Instead, the spotlight is on emotions that activate *reliable facial muscles.* This is also an Ekman concept and he claimed that activity of them communicates the presence of specific emotions.[17] As a corollary, the theory is that spontaneous activation of reliable facial muscles is really hard, if not impossible, to suppress.

A team of researchers from the University of Geneva tested Ekman's theory. They concluded that the reliable muscles "may indeed convey trustworthy information about emotional processes."[18] But there was a caveat: The researchers also concluded that these muscle activations were shared by several emotions rather than characteristic of just one.

For your purposes in spotting a deviation from baseline, the important thing is this: You're seeing something you hadn't seen before and your source couldn't help himself. Something you said triggered an involuntary response.

According to the researchers, the spontaneous response is likely to convey one of the following emotions. Several reliable muscles may be involved; a non-technical description of some muscles the person can't control, and what they're doing, are listed next to the emotion:

▶ Hot anger—margin of the lip tightened.

▶ Panic fear—lip stretched.

▶ Elation/joy—lip corner pulled.

▶ Sadness—lip corner depressed.

There is further discussion of facial expression in Chapter 8 in terms of what the emotion information tells you about how to extract the truth from source who is trying to hide something.

Arms and Legs

In observing arms, legs, and the body parts they are attached to, it's useful to talk in terms of concepts defined and popularized by Gregory Hartley, with whom I wrote several books on body language and interpersonal skills: illustrators, regulators, barriers, and adaptors.

▶ **Illustrators** are movements that punctuate a statement.

▶ **Regulators** are movements used to regulate another person's speech.

▶ **Barriers** are postures and objects that put separation between you and another person.

▶ **Adaptors** are actions that release stress.

The way people usually move their arms and legs to illustrate or accent a point can vary greatly depending on cultural norms. Those customs and habits may be shared by a nation, a gang, a club, or a family. It's not the size of the group that matters as much as its influence on behavior. The variance in what is "normal" is therefore a big reason why you need to observe an individual objectively to determine his baseline. Assuming that he's emotional about a situation just because his gestures are more outgoing than yours, for example, is flawed thinking.

So with illustrators, watch how the person moves her arms, stands, crosses her legs, and so on while she's under little or no stress. Deviations from whatever is typical for her—and that could be more or less expressive movements—signal that she's no longer in a relaxed state.

Regulators tend to be deliberate movements that you use to encourage someone to continue talking, try to speed up the conversation, or perhaps stop it altogether. A person in a relaxed state will probably use regulators such as nodding the head when listening to another person talking. Signals of impatience when someone is talking—taking a step toward a door, for example—indicate tension. In the situation where you are the one talking and asking your source questions, watch the person to note if he's doing anything that suggests "Hurry up! I want you to stop talking so I can get out of here!"

People often use barriers when they are uncomfortable. Watch people at a reception or other social event where they are meeting for the first time, or perhaps don't know each other well. You will see men and women clutching a glass with both hands and holding it in front of them. People will hold their plate of cheese and crackers directly in front of them as they are talking with another person. Look around the room and observe people in animated conversation—people who seem to know each other. They may be drinking, but the bottle of beer is in one hand while the other hand is gesturing, or the cheese plate is resting on a table and the person is using both hands to illustrate something he's saying.

These same differences can be seen in myriad professional situations. Whether the barrier is an object, such as a cell phone or laptop, or a body posture, such as arms crossed in front of the body, the person is exhibiting some level of discomfort. In the course of vetting your source, watch for any change in the way the body or an object is used to come between you and the person.

Adaptors are nervous, self-soothing gestures you do without thinking. They can make other people feel uncomfortable around you, but if you ask them, they might not even be able to tell you exactly why they feel uncomfortable. When you are asking a person questions to determine level of truthfulness, even if you've established a good rapport with him, the questions may make the person feel ill at ease. That doesn't mean what you hear next will be laced with deception, but it does mean that something you said has caused his stress level to rise.

Fingers and Toes

The extremities are far away from the brain when you compare them to facial muscles. They are less in your control, therefore, than your mouth or eyebrows are. If you want to see signs of stress leaking from someone's body, watch his or her extremities because most adaptors involve fingers and toes. Women tend to use relatively small movements, such as rubbing their fingertips together, touching their hair, playing with an earring, and wiggling their toes. Men may wring their hands, click a pen, or drum their fingers on a table.

In the course of the first book we did together, *How to Spot a Liar*, Greg Hartley told me that it wasn't uncommon for someone in one of his interrogation classes to signal intent with his feet and toes. He would sit a student in a chair at the front of the classroom for an exercise, which could be something psychologically challenging involving questioning skills or rapport-building. He said it was rather common for the student's toes to be pointed toward the door.

Throughout this section, the focus has been on the source's baseline and deviations from it. But the concept of detecting deviations from baseline can be viewed in two ways: from the point of view of the questioner and the point of view of the person answering questions.

▸ From the questioner's perspective, deviations suggest that the person's *presentation* of the answer reflects stress. Does evaluation of the *content* either confirm or refute suspicions?

▸ From the source's perspective, deviations suggest that the questioner has some stress associated with what he is asking. He has emotional attachment to it, and that emotion is leaking out.

The scan from eyes to toes from the previous sections provided insights into deviations from baseline. Some of those deviations are subtle. Here is a list of sample deviations that are more obvious and should trigger an immediate awareness that the person is under stress:

▶ Becoming more or less fidgety.

▶ Stiffening of posture.

▶ Use of noteworthy adaptors that involve self-preening, such as adjusting a tie or scarf or seeming to brush lint off a jacket, or self-soothing, such as massaging the neck.

▶ Shift in pitch, voice, or pace of speech.

▶ Use of fillers such as "um," as though the person needs time to think about what to say next.

These kinds of specific changes in voice and body get a closer examination in Chapter 8.

Red Flags in Real Life

When I first saw Brian Williams's interview with Edward Snowden, my response as someone who has studied verbal communication for decades and non-verbal communication for more than 10 years was, "He's deceitful." I made notes about why I felt so distrustful of Snowden and wondered what the scuttlebutt was in the ever-growing community of communication experts.

I discovered there were lots of people who disagreed with me. I also discovered that the preponderance of credentialed experts felt as I did: The interview proved him to be a liar.

Earlier in this chapter, I cited a couple of instances in which yes or no questions went unanswered. Those were among the verbal signs that Snowden had a script running in his head, with "yes" and "no" not being answers he wanted to give. He wanted to convey particular information, not give a definitive response. It was the same with his response about why he ended up in Russia: It was a slide-slip that evaded the reality that his passport was revoked prior to boarding the plane in Hong Kong for Russia, so questions remain as to why he was allowed to board the flight.

Similarly, his non-verbal communication seemed scripted to me. Dr. Nick Morgan, who has written extensively about the subject of non-verbal communication for *Forbes*, expresses the same first impression I had about the way Snowden sat. He began with his legs far apart, with feet planted firmly at the edge of the chair: "It came off as either genuinely deliberate or trained."[19] Later on the in the interview, he had one leg thrown over the other, with the right foot at the left knee in a figure-four. It's a very manly pose in Western society, conveying confidence or even arrogance. During the remainder of the interview, he alternated between the two leg positions.

Other indications include:

▶ Williams's question about ending up in Russia evoked a snicker and evasive eye movement.

▶ At a number of points in the interview, notably when Williams asked him about self-perception—noble whistleblower or hideous traitor—Snowden pursed his lips. Janine Driver, president of the Body Language Institute and a partner of Lena Sisco's in body language instruction, cautions: "When we don't like what we see or hear, our lips disappear. When we see notorious liars or people holding something back, their lips will disappear."[20]

In this reality check, I'd agree with Nick Morgan, who concluded that Snowden's body language suggests a "willed performance." He adds, "I wouldn't trust anything the man said.... There is something else going on here."[21]

In the upcoming chapters, you find out how intelligence pros forge relationships with the sources they've vetting—like them or not, and trust them or not—and then take them down a conversational path to get the sources to level with them.

There are traits—some ethnic, perhaps, and some the result of upbringing—that predispose certain people to be gifted at connecting with others and eliciting information. For the same reasons, other people have no gift for these things and it would be harder for them to cultivate rapport-building skills.[1]

—Elizabeth Bancroft,
executive director of the
Association of Former
Intelligence Officers

People who know me always call me Peter. When people call me Edwin—my legal first name—I know they are either selling insurance or running for office. You would think people in those professions would have done some homework before they try to connect with me.[2]

—E. Peter Earnest,
former Senior CIA National
Clandestine Service Officer and
executive director of the
International Spy Museum

Lyndon Johnson, the 36th President of the United States, famously noted that the "most tragic error" of his administration "may have been our inability to establish a rapport and a confidence with the press."[3] As a result, Johnson stated that he did not think the press understood him and, as a corollary, did not publish or broadcast the truth of what the administration undertook and accomplished.

In expressing this concern, Johnson suggested that historical records may therefore suffer from his failure to build rapport. The same can be said for our personal histories. Knowing how to build rapport is the foundation for leaving a legacy of truth.

Maslow's Folly

Everyone has needs, doubts, and insecurities. That is the first concept you need to embrace in honing your skills of rapport-building. The process of establishing a connection to another person to gain trust—and truth—centers on showing respect as you address his or her needs, doubts, and insecurities.

In 1943, psychologist Abraham Maslow published a paper titled "A Theory of Human Motivation," in which he described a hierarchy of needs, often depicted as shown on page 69.

The premise is that, unless "deficiency needs"—those on the lower part of the pyramid that have to do with survival and security—are met, then an individual will not be motivated to fulfill "growth needs."

Maslow had some valid things to say but wasn't completely correct, according to 21st-century behavioral science. And so, the art and skill of rapport-building has morphed, perhaps not so much in *what* people do with their sources to motivate them to tell the truth, but *why* they do it. A battlefield interrogator who wanted to build rapport with a prisoner, for example, may have begun the process by making sure he had something to eat and a sense that he would not be physically abused. He might still do that, but rather than view the actions primarily as ways to address deficiency needs, he would do them to demonstrate respect for the other person. The difference is more than a nuance; the latter recognizes that what means most to the individual is being respected and not simply being more physically comfortable.

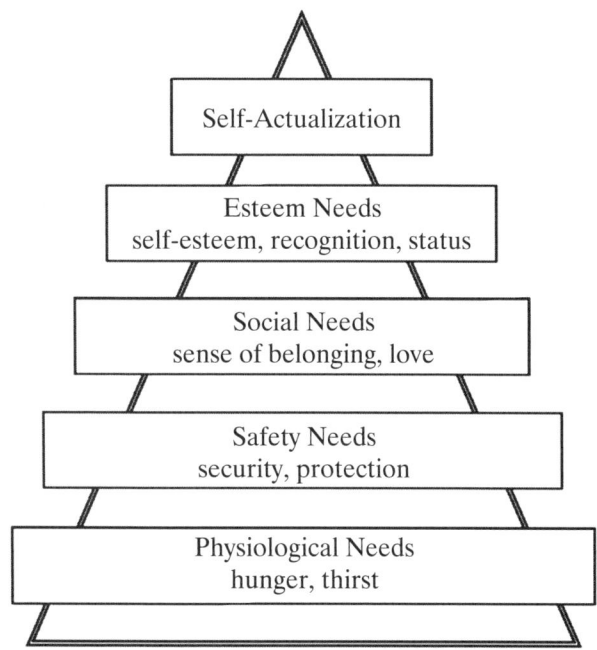

Researchers in various fields have taken different approaches that explored aspects of the question "What motivates people?" In 2011, University of Illinois researchers Louis Tay and Ed Deiner published results of five-year, multi-cultural study that directly put Maslow's hierarchy to the test. Their paper, published in the *Journal of Personality and Social Psychology*, was titled "Needs and Subjective Well-Being Around the World." Two questions at the heart of their study were: "Is the association of specific needs with subjective well-being dependent on the fulfillment of other needs?" and "Are needs typically fulfilled in the order described by Maslow?" One of their main conclusions was this: "A person can gain well-being by meeting psychosocial needs regardless of whether his or her basic needs are fully met."

Mutual of Omaha has a series of commercials they call "A-ha Moments." One of them is a touching story of man trying to help a homeless person. He asks, "What do you need?" The man says he just wants him to shake his hand. This is anecdotal evidence that pairs well with academic research asserting that the desire to connect is more powerful than the desire for food or safety.

The Scharff Method

When you have the skills of rapport-building—to make another person feel connected to you—you can even turn a hostile source into someone who interacts with you in a productive way. This is what Hanns Scharff did; he is the German Luftwaffe interrogator whose psychological techniques of connecting positively with prisoners have shaped U.S. non-physical interrogation practices in modern times.

Sharff was a self-taught interrogator who became fluent in English before the war while working in South Africa. Prisoners expected harsh, Gestapo-style treatment when they were marched into the room at Dulag Luft POW Camp, where they would be interrogated by him. Instead, they met a man who would soon draw out of them far more than name, rank, and serial number.

Key features of the Sharff method, which partially depended on the fact that prisoners were held in solitary confinement upon their arrival at the camp, included Sharff's own preparation, reinforcement of the prisoners' sense of insecurity, and establishing a respectful and comforting connection that relieved their sense of isolation.

▶ He tried to know everything possible about the prisoner before the interrogation began. He collected information about the pilot's military service, as well as his personal circumstances. He wove in such things as travel times from one place to another that would be familiar to the prisoner. Sharff's homework and insertion of relevant details into his conversation with prisoners helped him create the illusion that he knew a great deal about their military activities. It was psychologically disarming to prisoners who assumed he knew more than he did, so they were inclined to disclose information. It also laid a strong foundation for building rapport. Not only did Scharff speak English, but he also seemed to have a familiarity with their lives, values, and situations.

▶ He made it clear to the prisoner that working with him and the Luftwaffe was far preferable to being labeled a spy, with his fate then being in the hands of the Gestapo. The message kept prisoners off balance a bit, reminding them they were vulnerable, and at the same time gave them a reason to draw closer to Sharff.

▶ He displayed friendship. He went for walks in the
   woods with the men, took them to the zoo, and gave
   them flights in a German fighter plane. Depending
   on the environment and how that engendered certain kinds of conversation, the prisoners leaked
   myriad types of information, from social habits of
   military personnel to aircraft capability.

Sharff claimed that his rapport-building skills enabled
him to obtain information from 90 percent of all prisoners.[4]
Mastering techniques such as those used by Sharff positions
you perfectly to get the truth from someone.

Causes of Resistance

At the heart of these positive rapport-building techniques,
there is perception of what motivates people to *resist* a connection to another person, even though that may be the very thing
they seek. Here are some reasons why you and your source
may have some significant barriers to making a connection:

▶ One or both parties perceive that there is no
   shared value system or standards of morality. For
   example, Scharff represented an ideological opposite to his prisoners. His stood for a regime that
   was morally abhorrent to them. Similarly, people
   entrenched in different political parties may have
   zero motivation to connect.

▶ The source feels as though the person asking questions doesn't have a positive relationship with his
   team or friends; therefore, important relationships
   aren't getting the respect they deserve. This is a
   relatively common situation in a workplace where
   senior staff members, or bosses, are "them" and
   everyone else is "us." When one of "them" asks

questions of people working for him, they are not inclined toward the kind of interaction that engenders trust or leads to the truth.

▶ Negative emotions dominate. When Allied pilots first met Scharff, they had just gone through the shock and humiliation of capture, and then were thrown into solitary confinement. Initially, they were emotionally blocked from connecting with their interrogator no matter how nice he seemed. And think about how hard it could be for someone who had been traumatized by a doctor as a child to trust doctors as an adult. Even in a critical-care situation, he might not feel comfortable telling a doctor the truth.

Before trying to establish rapport with someone from whom you are seeking the truth, consider if there might be such ideological, social, or emotional barriers that will make your task very difficult.

Another barrier to true rapport is a threat. In some circumstances within law enforcement, military interrogation, and similar circumstances involving a suspect, the questioner may try a negative approach to building rapport. In other words, the connection may come out of desperation because the suspect feels threatened. This chapter doesn't explore those techniques, nor are they advocated anywhere in this book. A bond shaped by intimidation is not the most effective way to get the truth. You might get a few facts, but if a person's only reason for giving you information is that he's is a state of fear, he'll hold something back. Information is the only protection he has that you won't fire him, beat him up, or throw him in jail, so why would he give you the whole truth?

10 Rapport-Building Techniques

The Congruency Group's Lena Sisco, also referenced
in Chapter 2 (about reading body language to vet sources),
teaches "Top Ten Rapport Building Techniques," which bring
a Sharff-like approach into our 21st-century, everyday circumstances. Before going into them, however, note that the "R" in
her REBLE approach to reading body language is an important precursor.

Relaxing is necessary preparation for achieving your objective of establishing rapport to get the truth. Sisco offers a caution about the importance of relaxation in conveying a positive
first impression: "The minute you feel stupid is the minute
your look stupid. Feeling nervous or anxious causes your body
to go through particular physiological responses. Rapid heart-
beat, hard swallowing, stuttering, slouching—it all happens
and people can't control [these responses]. Before the body
gets to that fight-or-flight state, you have to relax yourself."[5]

The way to do a state transformation to be more relaxed
is through power poses and breathing. To a great extent, your
sense of relaxation reflects how confident you feel. What you
do with your body affects how you feel about yourself. I've
done an exercise for this with many people, and they understand quickly how the way you move your body affects how
you feel at the moment. If you keep reinforcing a positive and
confident state with your body language, the effect will be
long-lasting.

Exercise: Changing Your State

Think of something that makes you feel down, but not
downright depressed. Maybe someone said something he
meant to be funny, but you were humiliated by the "joke."
Even though you forgive the person, every time you think of
his remark, you feel a little emotional pain.

Plant that insult firmly in your head. Water it with your feelings of resentment and hurt.

Immediately get up and walk with a bounce in your step and your head held high. Smile at anyone you pass, and if you don't pass a human being, then smile at your cat.

How do you feel now?

You can't just walk down a hall and smile at people every time you feel emotionally weak and lack confidence, of course. Another way to accomplish your goal is to assume a *power pose*. Sisco recalls, "One company hired me to attend a networking meeting in which each of the 40 participants had to stand up for 45 seconds and do a self-introduction. Everyone had T-Rex arms." Sisco was referencing the fact that  everyone's arms were tucked into their sides so that they looked like the little, dangling arms of a T-Rex.

So while confident words came out of their mouths, their bodies indicated they were not confident. "When your arms are tucked in like that, it's like you're giving yourself a little hug."[6] In other words, it's an obvious self-soothing gesture, a physical way of telling ourselves, "I'm going to get through this; it'll be okay."

In contrast, a power pose looks like this:

▶ Your arms are comfortably at your side, with your body open to the person you're speaking with, and you use the whole arm in making a point.

▶ You're standing erect with your feet about six to 10 inches apart.

It can also look like this: Your arms are up the air, your chin is up, and you have a giant smile on your face. You can do it sitting or standing. It's the power pose you use in the elevator before you have a job interview, or the power pose you assume in the bathroom before you do a presentation to 200 people.

Does a power pose really make difference to your state of mind, as the exercise suggests? Yes. Unequivocally, yes.

Amy Cuddy is a professor at Harvard Business School whose research on body language focuses both on how we change other people's perceptions of us as well as how we bio-chemically can change ourselves. In one of her experiments, she opened with saliva samples of all subjects to determine their levels of the hormones testosterone and cortisol. The higher the testosterone level, the greater the subject's feeling of power; the higher the cortisol level, the more stress he or she felt. Next, she had some subjects adopt power poses for two minutes and other subjects adopt postures that suggested subservience and weakness. All the subjects were then asked how powerful they felt about a series of items. Next, they were offered the opportunity to gamble. Among those who had adopted the power poses, 86 percent chose to gamble. Only 60 percent of the subjects in the other group chose to gamble. Cuddy calls this a "whopping, significant difference."[7] The final phase of the experiment involved collecting another saliva sample to determine whether or not there was any discernible difference in the levels of testosterone and cortisol. The power posers had an average of a 20-percent rise in their testosterone levels; the low-power people experienced a 10-percent decrease. The high-power people experienced an average of a 25-percent decrease in cortisol levels; the weak posers experienced a 16-percent increase. These dramatic changes occurred after they spent just *two minutes* in the different types of poses!

My favorite story about the transformational power of positive body language comes from Cuddy's memorable TED talk called "Your Body Language Shapes Who You Are."[8] When she was 19, Cuddy suffered a serious brain injury in a car accident. When she woke up in the hospital, she learned she had been withdrawn from college and that her IQ had dropped by two standard deviations, or approximately 30 points. Part of Cuddy's identity was being smart; she had been labeled gifted as a child. She kept trying to go back to college despite people around her expressing their concern by discouraging her from inevitable failure.

Cuddy persevered and graduated from college four years after her peers. With that unlikely success behind her, she began the path toward a PhD in social psychology. This is the rest of the story in her words:

> I convinced someone, my angel advisor, Susan Fiske, to take me on, and so I ended up at Princeton, and I was like, *I am not supposed to be here. I am an impostor.* And the night before my first-year talk—and the first-year talk at Princeton is a 20-minute talk to 20 people, that's it—I was so afraid of being found out the next day that I called her and said, "I'm quitting." She was like, "You are not quitting, because I took a gamble on you, and you're staying. You're going to stay, and

this is what you're going to do. You are going to fake it. You're going to do every talk that you ever get asked to do. You're just going to do it and do it and do it, even if you're terrified and just paralyzed and having an out-of-body experience, until you have this moment where you say, 'Oh my gosh, I'm doing it. I have become this. I am actually doing this.'" So that's what I did.[9]

The message she now gives to students at Harvard who are similarly struggling is to "fake it until you become it." Practice the power poses for two-minute stretches and breathe like you own all the air in the world.

Now that you're relaxed and feeling supremely confident, simply apply Sisco's 10 techniques and you are well on your way to establishing rapport:

1. **Smile with your eyes.**
    It's the look you give to someone you are genuinely happy to see—a genuine smile with wrinkle lines, not the one that you see many celebrities use on the red carpet. Here's an example of smiling with the eyes (right).

2. **Use touch carefully.**
    Haptics is the study of communication by touch. Researchers in this field have found that students evaluated a library and its staff more favorably if the librarian briefly touched the patron while returning his or her library card, that female restaurant servers received larger tips when they

touched patrons, and that people were more likely to sign a petition when the petitioner touched them during their interaction.[10] Often when you meet people, you shake their hand. That's just the beginning. At some point in the conversation, you may want to use a gentle touch on the arm, for example. It's a physical reminder of the bond that's forming. Note that in some cultures, this would be inappropriate. Know your audience.

3. **Share something with the person about yourself.** The discussion of *quid pro quo* as a conversation motivator in Chapter 4 goes into this a little more. Basically, if you want to know about someone's job satisfaction, for example, you might volunteer that your boss is a perfectionist who is very difficult to please. The person is likely to feel you've divulged a secret and thus will be more forthcoming about his own workplace circumstances.

4. **Mirror the other person.** People like people who seem to be like them. Be cautious, however, because you do not want to mimic the other person; that will destroy rapport. Mirroring is subtle, such as a slight lean in the same direction as the other person or using an arm position that's similar. There is a verbal corollary to these kinds of mirroring movements. When you hear where a person is from or what baseball team he likes, you want to look for a connection, such as "My favorite cousin lives there" or "That was my dad's favorite team, too."

5. **Treat everyone with respect.** If you expect to be treated with respect by others, then that's how you have to treat them. Sisco discussed the emotional challenge of establishing rapport with members of the Taliban who had done horrific things to people. Her job as a military interrogator

depended on the ability to connect with them with respect; she had to remind herself, "At the end of the day, they are still human beings. They breathe oxygen just like I do. Every human being on the planet wants to be treated with respect, regardless of who they are or what they've done. To get them to talk to me, they have to feel honest respect from me."[11]

6. **Reinforce trust through your body language.** Use open body language, especially as it relates to the three power zones: nape of the neck, naval, and crotch. If you have your three power zones open to people, your body is projecting this message: "I'm open to you. I trust you."

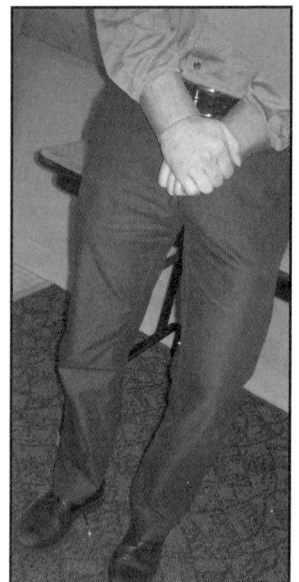

Consider the effect of the opposite—that is, covering each of these areas. As the photo indicates, there is a definite sense that the person feels either ill-at-ease or suggests that he is closed off from the person he's with—not perceptions that support rapport-building.

7. **Suspend your ego.** Show interest when the person tries to tell you how to do something or explains a concept to you. Let him educate you. People like to get on the soapbox. It makes them feel smart and important. This tip, along with the next one, is explored in greater depth in the Chapter 4 discussion of conversation motivators under "Boosting Ego."

8. **Flatter and praise.** It's not a matter of overtly buttering up the person, but rather just pleasantly offering a compliment about her accomplishments or family, for example. If you don't make someone feel good, why would she invest the time and trust in developing a rapport with you? Compliments energize people.

9. **Take your time to listen.** And by listen, I mean listen with your body. Lean into the person a little; nod your head at key points. When someone thinks that you have drifted away from the conversation, you've lost rapport. As part of your active listening, start using the other person's words when it makes sense. For example, you have no military background, but your subject is a Navy officer. He talks about ships, not boats. So you talk about ships, not boats. Adopting keywords shows you are paying attention.

10. **Get your subject talking *and* moving.** Ask open-ended questions requiring a narrative response. These are questions that begin with an interrogative: who, what, when, where, how, and why. Jim Pyle and I devoted an entire book to the art and skill of using such questions in *Find Out Anything From Anyone, Anytime.* As a companion to talking, when you move the conversation from one place to another you have set the stage for truly energizing your rapport-building. Remember the reference earlier in this chapter to Hanns Scharff's technique of taking prisoners for walks in the woods or accompanying them to a trip to the local zoo. If you're interviewing someone for a job, for example, walk the person from your office to the elevator as you continue to talk. Once a person has had the experience of connecting with you in different environments, the bond between you strengthens.

Going Global With Rapport

Global consciousness is also a significant part of the 21st-century conversation about rapport-building. The following story is from Michael T. Reilly, currently a deputy chief fire marshal in Fairfax County, Virginia, and a reserve special agent in the Coast Guard Investigative Service (CGIS). It illuminates how rapport can be instantly destroyed by a deficiency in cultural sensitivity:

> I was stationed in the Middle East, doing some training for the Royal Saudi Police Academy. I was part of a team teaching a post-blast emergency medical response program for Saudi national police officers who were going to be responding to bombings and other acts of violence. One of the classes was on cardiopulmonary resuscitation (CPR) and the Heimlich maneuver.
>
> The first problem we had was that we gave them a bunch of Annies, which are training mannequins used for teaching CPR. That was our first mistake. You would have thought I had chopped Mohammed's head off right there in the office.
>
> Resuscitator Annie [aka Resusci Annie or CPR Annie] has breasts. Touching the manikin's breast areas is *harām*—that is, forbidden by Allah. It is a sinful act.
>
> We had to have a *Muttawa* (religious police) come in and tell the Saudi troops that it was okay to work on the manikin.[12]

Reilly's learning about how to connect with his Saudi students continued. What he experienced is extreme, but the rest of us experience versions of this every day. People have experiences that shape their concepts of what is right and what is truth. If we don't recognize and respect the significance of those experiences, the probability of forging a trusting connection is extremely low.

He was trying to teach one of the dignitary protection officers the Heimlich maneuver, which are abdominal thrusts designed to dislodge food stuck in the trachea that's causing the victim to choke to death. These are people charged with protecting the lives of the Saudi royal family. The session with Reilly went like this:

We demonstrated the Heimlich maneuver and he said, "I do not need to know this."

I said, "Yes, you do. If the prince or king has an airway obstruction, you going to need to perform the Heimlich maneuver."

"No, I would not do that."

"What do you mean?"

"You do not understand. If I do that and I did not remove the object and the prince or king died, then my head would be cut off the next day."

I grasped the concept quickly that he would be beheaded if he failed in executing the maneuver. So I took a slightly different approach to teaching. "Suppose one of your children is choking. Wouldn't you want to know how to save him?"

In straight-faced candor, he said, "I can have another."[13]

Reilly learned to remove his judgment from the interaction. He had an acute awareness that *respect* for the other person's values and sensibilities held the key to forging a connection with him. Not only that, but Reilly realized that respect for the man's national pride, cultural heritage, and religious beliefs—everything feeding those values and sensibilities—was essential in rapport-building.

Going Online With Rapport

There are three angles to the discussion of going online to establish and reinforce rapport: online resources that are useful in all forms of rapport building—face-to-face, phone, and written—best practices for building rapport electronically, and rapport-wrecking actions.

Online Resources

Online resources enable you to do three things that support rapport-building:

1. Find out facts about a person's history, such as previous jobs, education, where he's lived, what clubs and groups he belongs to (in real life or online), and much more.

2. Use the information you discovered to pinpoint areas where your interests and experiences intersect and/or are in sync. The more a person feels she has something in common with you, the easier it will be to establish rapport.

3. Contact the person in a non-intrusive way, inviting a response to form a connection, but not requiring it in the same way as if you showed up at his office and introduced yourself.

In the discussion of what Hanns Scharff did to forge connections with Allied prisoners of war, I noted that he did his homework about the individuals he intended to interrogate. Social media sites offer you goldmines of information about people so that you can do the kind of homework that helps you strengthen an initial interaction. You can find out enough to make your connection with them can feel personal. You can find out how best to present yourself so that your outreach makes sense to the person, whether that outreach is in writing, on the phone, or in person.

Before approaching someone, you first want to find out what networks he belongs to and what groups within those networks. For example, one of the people I interviewed for this book is David Major, a leading authority on counterintelligence. Before meeting with him, I researched his background on LinkedIn, so I could demonstrate that I cared enough about the interview to know not only what he studied in college (biochemistry), but also to be aware of what boards he serves on (International Spy Museum and Association of Former Intelligence Officers). I also took note that his connections included a number of people that I should probably interview for the book.

Major is not on Facebook. However, another of the key people I interviewed for the book is on Facebook, as well as LinkedIn and Twitter: Lena Sisco. Knowing that we had professional associates in common (through LinkedIn), as well as similar tastes in movies and a love of animals (through Facebook), I had a keen sense of how we might interact. Julio Viskovich, whose expertise is primarily helping people to drive sales with social media, notes that "using social media will allow you to align yourself with your audience, give you a common interest, and allow you to demonstrate value based on your assessment before meeting."[14]

But the kinds of searches that yield this worthwhile information can be time consuming as you move from site to site. An online resource that reduces that research time is Nimble, which pulls your contacts into one place automatically. It also provides a dashboard of daily activities across your networks, and you can receive reminders about staying in touch with members of your network—so-called engagement opportunities. As the social media world gets more complex, Nimble is the kind of tool that has a lot of value in understanding and managing relationships.

Best Practices

Long before the World Wide Web linked us to people around the planet, best practices of intelligence organizations, exclusive clubs, and socially adept hosts foreshadowed the kind of actions and information that facilitate rapport-building. These are practices that promote a sense of trust, respect, and consideration.

The historical and anecdotal information about best practices in the upcoming paragraphs illustrates how you can take the same kinds of actions by thoughtfully using social media and other online resources.

Connect with a person, not a number.

Throughout the ages, many clubs have required that one or more current members give their word that a candidate for membership maintains the personal and/or professional standards that the group values. The Freemasons state: "A well-recommended person is one for whom another is willing to vouch."[15] Some organizations insist on an even more intimate connection. For example, when a colleague of mine sought membership in San Francisco's Olympic Club, a private social club and the oldest athletic club in the United States, the person who vouched for him was asked if he had ever had my friend to his home, which was an essential part of the vetting process.

The core message of the best practice is, therefore, that your designation of someone as a trusted friend, ally, or colleague cannot mean that person is perceived as one of many. Your "club" must be exclusive; a person must meet certain standards to get into it. If people in your circle have reason to believe that, you have leverage with them when it comes to truth-telling.

A lot of people look at Facebook, LinkedIn, and Twitters as numbers games. That's good for some purposes and terrible for others. If you're thinking about getting a book published, the publisher will take a look at your connections and followers to ascertain whether you seem to have the ability to drive sales of your book. There's a downside, though, in terms of your perceived value as a connection if you hit high numbers by saying yes to everyone. Keeping the discussion focused on your ability to vouch for someone, or another person's ability to vouch for you, I'd caution you that having thousands of connections undermines the perception that you choose friends and colleagues carefully. It is not a best practice.

Why? Remember that your ability to establish trust and rapport has to do with how the other person perceives you and how much you have in common, not precisely what you do or who you are. This is why sociopaths with brilliant social skills can be so successful in business, politics, and other fields. They are not trustworthy, nor do they necessarily share interests or values with their target audiences, but they are perceived by them as having what it takes to be a colleague, friend, or desirable leader. Facebook is not very different when it comes to perception, according to the team of researchers who authored "Too Much of a Good Thing? The Relationship Between Number of Friends and Interpersonal Impressions on Facebook," which was published in the *Journal of Computer-Mediated Communication.* They concluded: "[J]udgments of social attractiveness are due to similarity of the rater to the target."[16] Given that the average number of friends is around 300, they found evidence to substantiate that the optimum number of friends to inspire a sense of intimacy and genuine connections is about the same. In summary, they said:

> This study advances the important finding that socio-metric data such as the number of friends one has on Facebook can prove to be a significant cue by which individuals make social judgments about others in an online social network. This study contributes findings that in the case of social attractiveness and extraversion, individuals who have too few friends or too many friends are perceived more negatively than those who have an optimally large number of friends.[17]

In short, this is an issue of quality and the right quantity. High numbers of connections may give you the illusion of closeness, but that's all it is—an illusion.

Use your online resources to help you make people feel special.

There are plenty of historical illustrations of this, with a particularly memorable one coming out of the Cold War between the Soviet Union and the United States.

Polish colonel Ryszard Kuklinski defected to the United States in 1972, and among the important pieces of information he gave the CIA in the next nine years were the secret plans to crush solidarity. Throughout those years, he took enormous risks, jeopardizing his life and that of his family. But from the very first meeting with his CIA handler to his dramatic escape to the West, the CIA took steps to recognize his humanity as well as the value of his contributions.

At his first meeting with Kuklinski, David Forden—code-named Daniel—explained why the CIA was involved and introduced him to the tradecraft that would be part of their operations. He also wished Kuklinski a belated happy birthday, letting him know that the two of them were nearly the same age. The birthday wishes triggered an unexpected outpouring of thoughts and feelings:

> Kuklinski grabbed the microphone Daniel had placed on the table and spoke with great emotion and purposefulness. He thanked Daniel for his birthday wishes, which had meant a lot to him. On the General Staff, he said, birthdays were rarely celebrated; everyone was too busy. One day, a few years earlier, Kuklinski said, he had told a colleague that it was his fortieth birthday. "For me, it is a certain special moment—in the life of every man—40 years."
>
> His friend joked cynically, "We've already had our drink. Get your ass out of here and back to work!"
>
> Kuklinski laughed. It was typical of how people were treated on the General Staff, he said. "To a man from whom the last juices are sucked out." Any flicker of emotion or happiness was "extinguished." He added, "An individual counts nothing in our system."[18]

Sites such as Facebook make it easy to remember someone's birthday, so take advantage of it. Similarly, when you see that one of your LinkedIn connections got a promotion or a new job, congratulate that person. One of my colleagues is also very good about thanking people for endorsing him on LinkedIn, and those expressions of appreciation have paid off for him in new consulting opportunities. All of these ostensibly small gestures strengthen rapport; they potentially expand the number of people who legitimately compose your trusted inner circle.

In conducting interviews for this book, I have learned that people who have these kinds of interactions on Facebook and LinkedIn are much more likely to feel a sense of confidence/trust in those people when they see them face-to-face than if they had not had the online interaction. They tell me that they jump into personal, confidential conversations much more readily than if they had not had the positive online contact.

Apply rules of etiquette to electronic communication.

One of the authors my literary agency represents is a gentleman in every sense of the word. His name is Ira Neimark, the former CEO of Bergdorf Goodman. Since 2005, we have exchanged thousands of e-mails and without fail, he begins with "Dear Maryann" and ends with "Best regards, Ira." I reply in kind—even if I am pecking out an e-mail on my iPhone. I feel honored, and perhaps even elevated, by his consistent courtesy. And in some way, no doubt subliminal most of the time, I feel as though he has earned my immediate attention on any range of issues. As a corollary, we trust each other.

The seconds that it takes to inject civility and respect into e-mails and texts yield a huge payout in terms of rapport-building. And part of being civilized is not making an assumption that the other person gets your sense of sarcasm, irony, or humor. Your tone of voice cannot be heard in an e-mail or text.

Rapport-Wrecking Actions

When electronic communication puts distance between you and another person, it's very hard to restore the sense of trust and rapport by using the e-mail or texting. Once the damage is done, you need to go face-to-face or at least have a phone call to add other dimensions of communication, such as tone of voice and non-verbal signals of openness.

With that thought in mind, consider these abuses of e-mail and text:

Relying solely on written, electronic communication like e-mail and text to manage a relationship is a mistake.

Even if you think you have a trusting relationship and really understand someone, it helps to at least phone occasionally or the rapport could weaken to the point of disappearing.

I had what I thought was a great relationship with a book editor to whom I introduced an aspiring author. The editor signed the author and then, three months later, the editor cancelled the publishing contract. I was shocked and sent the editor an e-mail asking what happened.

The note I got back did not strike me as the truth, even though I would have bet this person would never try to deceive me. I tried again via e-mail and got a similar answer, and I still wasn't satisfied. Something about the response seemed scripted, in contrast to the casual exchanges we usually enjoyed.

I called the editor, and she said that her boss had told her to say that the book didn't meet the company's standards, but the truth was that the business was running in the red so she was getting laid off and almost all her projects were getting axed. The e-mails captured the boss's words, and even the boss's personality, so my initial sense of being deceived had a foundation.

One phone conversation allowed us to get back on track. We realized what had just happened between us; it was distressing, as we'd become friends over the years. We promised each other that we would never go "all e-mail" again.

And if someone does something nice for you, do not use a texting to say thank you. That mode of expressing gratitude trivializes what the person did for you.

Texting is a valuable tool for spontaneous communication, but it turns ugly when the spontaneity is linked to anger.

This text exchange is real—typos and all—and in the same sequence received and sent; only the names have been changed to protect the identities of the people involved. The text messages took place between Nancy, a friend of mine, and her hair stylist of 10 years, Barb. Barb had also been doing housecleaning for her for the previous year. The hairstylist decided to use a new type of color on Nancy's hair the evening before she went on a business trip. The next morning, from the airport, Nancy sent her first message of concern:

Nancy: Too uniform. Does not look natural.

Barb: U r funny always uniform first day LOL Wait a
        shampoo or two!

My not-so-funny friend then called the stylist, who told her to wash her hair with Prell shampoo and baking soda. The situation did not improve.

Nancy: Barb—I continue to be very dissatisfied with my
        recent color. It has been seven days now and it still
        looks like it was put on with a can of spray paint.
        This is despite having washed it three times with
        Prell shampoo and baking soda. It looks unnatural.
        Over the weekend, I had someone I see regularly

comment for the first time that I must be coloring my hair. The reason I have you do my color is to achieve a natural look. If this result was acceptable to me I could just use products I can find at Safeway and save a lot of money. I do not ever want to experiment like this again when I have some high profile events immediately after a color. I also want a clear understanding of what I can expect before we ever change products or formulas again. For now, I want to return to what we have been using in the past that has provided acceptable results.—Nancy

Barb: Sorry Nancy but my prices have increased and colors are now $75 that's with a haircut affective immediately and so has my cleaning $25 with the vacuum, $30 with cleaning supplies... if there's any changes at your end please feel free to let me know! Thanks, Nancy—BARB

It seems inconceivable that someone in a customer service business would respond to an earnest complaint with a price increase, but this is what the stylist did. Every time my friend Nancy looked at her phone and read the message, she got angrier. The rapport they had was destroyed. Another factor to consider is that they both live in a small town, and it's highly likely someone will notice that my friend is now going to a different stylist.

Texting tends to be an unplanned, uncensored exchange, so if strong emotion is present, it will bleed out onto the screen. You have no guarantee that the recipient will glance at a text you typed while feeling grumpy and dismiss it as "Joe's just in a bad mood." The next time that person picks up his phone and receives a text from you, the grumpy-Joe text will probably still be there as a reminder that you have a bad side. Whether this occurs in the context of a personal relationship or a professional one, the effect can be corrosive.

Here is the key: Whether you forge a connection face-to-face, over the phone, or online, rapport-building *must* involve interaction. This is why Facebook, for example, is a useful tool, whereas any "push" communication is not.

First learn the meaning of what you say, and then speak.

—Epictetus

After decades of service in the field, Peter Earnest returned to the United States to continue to serve at CIA headquarters in Langley, Virginia. One of his assignments was covering the Senate staff for the CIA on Capitol Hill, and he became friendly with Mike Epstein, a staffer on the Senate Oversight Committee. When two women joined the committee as fellow staffers, Epstein told them, "You have to meet Peter Earnest. He's our main liaison to the CIA." He brought the women to Langley, where Peter chatted with them and gave them a tour of the lobby. On the way back in the car, the two women were talking about their experience. Peter recalls: "Mike told me that one of the women remarked, 'And Peter Earnest—wasn't he charming?' Mike said, 'Remember: He's paid to be charming.'"[1]

After the attacks in New York City and at the Pentagon on September 11, 2001, some CIA personnel didn't seem so charming when they were linked to physical abuses such as waterboarding. Nonetheless, for the most part, the image of a charismatic spy à la Sean Connery's James Bond has prevailed as the image of someone in the clandestine service.

Contrast this with the stereotypical persona of the military interrogator, trained to use the tools of fear and intimidation that one would never associate with a charming individual. In some ways, however, the two are close cousins. Both have skills in motivating conversation that, at their core, are very similar in nature.

In this chapter, I'll take a look at military and non-military ways we might talk about motivating conversations, including how they might be combined and how to match personal style with the motivators.

Military-Style Motivators

The U.S. Army Field Manual (FM) issued in 1992 listed 14 interrogation techniques, which are defined as approaches to help establish rapport. When you go through them, you'll realize that "rapport" is used in a broader sense than the way I've previously defined it—that is, an affinity for another person. In the context of a military interrogation, rapport may mean an understanding and cooperation that takes shape despite the reluctance or hostility of the source. Thinking in terms of military-style motivation as captured in the approaches can be useful when your source doesn't really want to come clean—a situation that is explored in Chapters 8 and 9 of the book.

When the FM was revised in September 2006, it listed 19 approaches, with two new ones requiring special approval from someone in command, and the other additions just variations on the themes already captured in the original group. The approaches with the official descriptions[2] (many paraphrased) are:

» **Direct:** The interrogator asks questions directly related to information sought, making no effort to conceal the interrogation's purpose.

» **Incentive:** The incentive approach is based on the application of inferred discomfort upon a source who lacks willpower. He wants something and will talk to get it. It could something immediate, such as having assurance that a buddy is okay, or it could be something more long-term, such as political asylum.

» **Emotional:** In the Field Manual of 2006, this became a category of approaches that encompasses seven different techniques. I think the earlier version has clearer distinctions, however, and will rely on those. In the previous FM, the emotional approach has two versions: emotional love and emotional hate. The interrogator uses verbal and emotional ruses in applying pressure to the source's dominant emotions.

  ▶ The **emotional love** approach is useful with a source who has a great love for his unit and fellow soldiers. The interrogator may take advantage of it by telling the source that by providing salient information, he may shorten the battle and save the lives of his friends.

  ▶ The **emotional hate** approach takes advantage of the inverse relationship of the source to his comrades. It could rise out of a feeling of being left behind to be captured, for example. The interrogator then gives him an opportunity for revenge.

» **Fear Up:** This approach is the exploitation of a source's pre-existing fear during the period of capture and interrogation—a fear that may be justified or unjustified. It's certainly justified if he knows that his captors saw him shoot one of their own.

▶ **Fear Up Mild** heightens fear by making the source realize the unpleasant consequences of not cooperating. It doesn't involve the yelling and banging that would characterize the fear up (harsh) approach.

▶ **Fear Up Harsh** involves displays of physical power and voiced threats. It does not mean that the interrogator perpetrates physical abuse, though.

» **Fear Down:** This technique is nothing more than calming the source and convincing him he will be properly and humanely treated, or telling him the war for him is mercifully over and he need not go into combat again.

» **Pride and Ego:** The strategy of this approach is to trick the source into revealing desired information by goading or flattering him. It's considered most effective with sources who have displayed weakness or feelings of inferiority.

▶ **Pride and Ego Up:** The source is constantly flattered into providing certain information in order to gain some kind of special benefit or credit. This is one instance when the Field Manual even provides body language cues that the approach is working. It instructs interrogators to watch for the source raising his head, getting a look of pride in the eyes, a swelling chest, and stiffening of the back.

▶ **Pride and Ego Down:** This approach is based on attacking the source's sense of personal worth. Any source who shows any real or imagined inferiority or weakness about himself or his loyalty to his unit, or perhaps was captured under embarrassing circumstances, would be a prime candidate for this approach.

» **Futility:** In this approach, the interrogator convinces the source that resistance to questioning is futile; she's just playing on doubts that already exist in the source's mind. It's a way of confirming that there is no way of escaping, reinforcing his suspicion that the battle is lost anyway and all of his buddies are in the same situation, or using any other scenario of hopelessness to get him to cooperate.

» **We Know All:** In this approach, the interrogator walks in with as much information as possible about the source. The problem is, unless he has enough to go on to sustain detailed questioning, the source will see right through him. There's another version of this called "file and dossier," which means the interrogator walks in with a paper file on the source. He might be flipping through blank pages, but he has to make it look like there is a lot of information. Even when the Field Manual was updated in 2006, this approach was described as involving a paper file, but one can only assume that with the proliferation of mobile devices and the disappearance of paper files, the model for "file and dossier" will change.

» **Establish Your Identity:** This is a great trap that law enforcement personnel use as well. The interrogator insists that the source has been correctly identified as an infamous individual wanted by higher authorities on serious charges, and that he is not the person he purports to be. In an effort to clear himself of this allegation, the source makes a genuine and detailed effort to establish or substantiate his true identity. In the process, he may provide the interrogator with information and leads for further development.

» **Repetition:** The interrogator repeats the question to erode resistance—sometimes through sheer boredom. An upscale version of this is rephrasing the question and repeating it.

» **Rapid Fire:** This approach involved a psychological ploy based on the principles that (1) everyone likes to be heard when he speaks, and (2) it's confusing to be interrupted mid-sentence with an unrelated question. One or two interrogators ask a series of questions in such a manner that the source doesn't have time to answer one completely before being driven to the next one. The source tends to contradict himself because he has no time to consider his answers thoughtfully; this gives the interrogator an opportunity to point out inconsistencies. In countering with information to explain himself, the source may end up releasing more than he had intended.

» **Silent:** The interrogator says nothing; he just makes unfliching eye contact with the source. It's normal human behavior to want to fill a void with words, so the source ultimately might say something like "What do you want from me?"

» **Change of Scene:** The idea in using this approach is to get the source away from the atmosphere of an interrogation room or setting. This was one of Scharff's techniques: He would take prisoners out for walks in the forest or even give them a ride in a German aircraft.

In addition, the two in the 2006 version of the FM that have to be authorized are:

▸ **Good Cop/Bad Cop,** which is also known as Friend and Foe, or Mutt and Jeff (the latter named after the comic strip characters who were physical opposites, one tall and the other short). This involves a team of two interrogators, one who is strict, or even harsh, and the other, sympathetic.

▶ **False Flag,** in which the interrogator tries to convince the source that he's been detained by forces other than U.S. forces; the idea is to get him to feel more inclined to cooperate with Americans.

In the following section, you will see how most of these approaches relate to the eight categories of conversation motivators that fit the mentality of a questioner who is not in the battlefield.

Non-Military Motivators

These conversation motivators have a foundation in military approaches and the psychological levers inherent in them, but the focus here is more broadly on human nature, neurobiology, and day-to-day applicability. In general, they also aren't meant to heighten the anxiety of a source—what I would call a "push approach"—but rather to draw the source toward you—a "pull approach."

In synthesizing all I've learned from various intelligence professionals, I have settled on eight motivators:

▶ Childlike curiosity.

▶ Incentives.

▶ Emotional appeal.

▶ Boosting ego.

▶ Deflating ego.

▶ Easing fears.

▶ Certainty/uncertainty.

▶ Silence.

Childlike Curiosity

A good questioner is purposeful and provocative. The questions lead somewhere and they stimulate interest in the person being questioned. In terms of seeking the truth, therefore, we can view curiosity as a two-way street. You are driven to know something, but the person who is your source of that information will probably have questions rushing through her brain as well: "Why do you want to know?" "Who told you I knew anything about this?" "What else do you want to know?" The list goes on and on. You can exploit the fact that your questions arouse curiosity in your source. You may be asking the questions, but those questions suggest you may know something that *she* wants to know, too.

Behavioral economist George Loewenstein did breakthrough studies of human curiosity and is probably best known for his gap theory of curiosity. He postulated that curiosity flourishes when we feel there is a gap in our knowledge; it's an itch we have to scratch. That chasm between what you know and what you want to know drives your questions.

Loewenstein begins a famous paper titled "The Psychology of Curiosity" by reminding us what a powerful role curiosity plays in our lives:

> Curiosity has been consistently recognized as a critical motive that influences human behavior in both positive and negative ways at all stages of the life cycle. It has been identified as a driving force in child development and as one of the most important spurs to education attainment…. Curiosity has also been cited as a major impetus behind scientific discovery, possibly eclipsing even the drive for economic gain.[3]

Broadcast journalists often have a five-days-a-week challenge of posing direct questions to guests they hope to engage, while sustaining the curiosity of listeners. They want people hearing the Q&A to crave the next question and feel satisfied at the end of the interview that some gap in their knowledge had been filled. Part of the job is choosing subjects that listeners and viewers care deeply about. When the broadcasters get it right, they exploit one of the most powerful determinants of curiosity: the intensity with which the audience wants to resolve their uncertainly about the issue.

Brian Williams's interview with Edward Snowden not only attempted to fill a knowledge gap about an issue that's inflaming passions, but also to create a narrative arc so viewers sensed that there was a story unfolding. After introducing the interview with the backstory of Snowden's release of classified documents, he began with a statement to which Snowden responded with a question. That opening gave the impression that this might be an interview filled with Snowden grandstanding unless Williams started charging hard down a path with his own questions—which he did.

Williams:　A lot of people would say you have badly damaged your country.

Snowden:　I'd say, can you show that? Is there any demonstration?

Shortly thereafter, the questions began and a story unfolded. Focusing on the relationship with Russia was like putting a pin into a map for viewers. Instead of a disembodied head, as he'd appeared in "live" interviews since his exile began, Snowden was a physical being located in a country with which the United States has tepid relations. The questions then got Snowden moving back and forth between actions and motivations, with Williams ratcheting up tension as he questioned. Then he zeroed in on what surveillance involving personal computers and mobile devices really means. Suddenly, it was our lives that were being discussed; we were in the story, and we cared—one way or the other—about what happened to Edward Snowden. The finale again gave us a pin on a map. Whistleblower or traitor, there he is in Russia, and chances are good that's where he'll stay for a while.

In short, curiosity is a vital tool in seeking the truth, regardless of what other motivators are employed.

Incentives

The U.S. Army manual references both short- and long-term incentives as techniques to gain cooperation, but that may not be as valid in day-to-day life as it is during war. Whereas political asylum may be a strong motivator for a prisoner of war, neuroscience tells us that human beings are more inclined to want immediate gratification rather than wait for an incentive that comes later—even if it's better than the quick choice.

A team of researchers that included the curiosity guru, George Loewenstein, as well as Jonathan Cohen, a Princeton University professor known for his study of decision-making, found that people don't like to delay their rewards. In one study, they had subjects undergo functional magnetic resonance imaging (fMRI) while considering certain incentives. They had a choice between Amazon.com gift certificates ranging from $5 to $40 in value, and certificates worth larger amounts that they could get only by waiting anywhere from two to six weeks. The brain scan indicated that decisions about the possibility of immediate reward activated parts of their brain associated with emotion. Consideration of the long-term option activated brain systems associated with reasoning. For a lot of people, the emotion-related parts of the brain won out over the reasoning-related parts of the brain.

Loewenstein explained, "Our results help explain how and why a wide range of situations that produce emotional reactions, such as the sight, touch or smell of a desirable object, often cause people to take impulsive actions that they later regret."[4] Psychological cues such as these trigger dopamine-related circuits in the brain similar to the ones that responded to immediate rewards in the study he did with Cohen. An interesting corollary to Lowenstein's conclusion relates to what he has said about curiosity as well, namely, that "curiosity is associated with behavior disorders such a voyeurism and has been blamed for nonsanctioned behaviors such as drug and alcohol use, early sexual experimentation, and certain types of crime."[5]

An important thing to note about the first two motivators, then, is that both often relate to satisfying a desire for something *as soon as possible.*

Another important link between them is that one of the strongest incentives is sometimes providing information that satisfies your source's curiosity. This is the foundation of the *quid pro quo,* a Latin phrase meaning "something for something."

Imagine that you are interviewing a young woman for a position in your company's human resources department. Although she has said that she adhered strictly to her current employer's company policies, you need to find out if her record is as flawless as she asserts. Your incentive to move her toward greater candor is to tell her a secret of yours. You mention that it's hard to do everything by the book all the time when you're dealing with human beings and their varied circumstances. You confess that at one point early in your career in HR, you stretched the definition of a sick day to allow an employee to be with her child on his fourth birthday. Her trust in you escalates because you opened up to her. She, in turn, tells you there were a couple of experiences during the three years she's been in HR that she has bent the rules to accommodate an employee need. You accomplished your mission to get a less-sanitized version of her job performance by using a straightforward *quid pro quo.*

Note that in this scenario, as in every judicious use of *quid pro quo,* the questioner gives up relatively inconsequential information as compared to that of the source. Leak your secrets thoughtfully so you retain control of the conversation.

Emotional Appeal

Move away from the military discussion of "love of" and "hate of" when it comes to emotion-related conversation motivators. Instead, think in terms of positive emotions and negative emotions and how you can use your awareness of them in others to get them to tell you the truth. Also think in terms of a desire for pleasure versus an aversion to punishment.

Aaron Ben-Zeév, one of the world's leading experts in the study of emotions, has looked closely at whether positive or negative emotions have greater importance in a person's life. His insights suggest that the answer is that, overall, positive emotions—especially love—have more importance, but there are plenty of situations in which the negative ones rule. There's a big reason why it may be easier to get your source to cooperate if he's motivated by anger, disgust, hurt, or anything else in the family of negative emotions: "People ruminate about events that induce strong negative emotions five times as long as they do about events that induce strong positive ones. Hence, it is no wonder that people tend to recall negative experiences more readily than positive ones."[6]

Ben-Zeév further explains that the reason why negative emotions may prevail over positive ones is that the repercussions of responding inappropriately to negative events exceed those of responding inappropriately to positive events, "since negative events can kill us while positive events will merely enhance our well-being."[7]

Reconfiguring the example of the young HR professional previously mentioned, we can come up with two scenarios wherein negative emotions play the critical role in her coming clean:

1. She's having a similar conversation with a senior executive at her company—her manager's boss. He suggests that some of the policies that the manager put in place are excessive and costing the company too much money to enforce. If he had any evidence that these policies were wasteful and unnecessary, he would order the manager to change them. The young HR professional dislikes her boss and finds she can't resist the temptation to share her violations of those very policies with the senior executive.

2. She's having a similar conversation with her boss, but this time, he suspects she has violated company policy and says simply, "To me, it's worse if someone lies than if there's a little step over the line. Frankly, I wouldn't hesitate to fire a liar." The statement does not give her a guarantee that if she comes clean about her transgressions that she will keep her job, but she knows that being caught in a lie will doom her. Being honest won't bring her pleasure, but it will potentially avert pain.

On the positive side of the equation, love is thought by many experts to be the most powerful motivator of all. But not just any love—the kind of love that stimulates the same reward centers of the brain as cocaine is romantic love, not selfless love like the kind the Sisters of St. Joseph gave us in elementary school. In fact, Yale University researchers found that the selfless brand of love—an abiding and sincere desire for others to be happy without any expectation of personal reward—actually turns off those same areas of the brain that romantic love turns on. It's the anti-fix.

Romantic love is an addiction, and we all know what diehard addicts will do to get a fix: anything. Sometimes "anything" means telling the truth.

Of course, romantic love and selfless love are not the only varieties of this emotion. There is a branch of study called interpersonal neurobiology, which is associated with Daniel J. Siegel and Allan N. Schore, colleagues at the University of California who explore what love looks like in the brain. Their work is premised on the fact that human relationships, from birth to death, alter our brain circuits related to memory and emotion.[8] From the time we're babies, we lay down neural patterns that affect our later behavior and choices.

How much or how little we respond to psychological levers related to love, therefore, has its roots in the degrees to which we felt linked to our mommy.

Boosting Ego

Scientific American began its January 12, 2010 article titled "Flattery Will Get You Far" with this paragraph:

> Here at *Scientific American* we understand the wisdom of our readership. Your intellect sets you apart from the rest of the population, and we are gracious to have you as visitors to this website. As someone of exceptional judgment, we know you will be interested

in subscribing to our exclusive online material, appropriate for only the most discerning intellectuals, and available to you for only \$9.99/month.[9]

You may choose to be cynical and say that this kind of supercilious junk doesn't work, but it does—time after time. In 2010, two Hong Kong University of Science and Technology researchers published a paper in the *Journal of Marketing Research* titled "Insincere Flattery Actually Works: A Dual Attitudes Perspective." The paper discusses when and how flattery is a tactic that makes people more positive about and cooperative with the source of compliments.

Elaine Chan and Jaideep Sengupta asked participants in their study to evaluate the merits of a new department store based on a store advertisement. The ad described what the store had to offer, praising readers for the kind of good taste and fashion sense that would draw them to the store. Study participants were not fooled; on a conscious level, they recognized that there was attempt to manipulate them in the same way the opening paragraph of the *Scientific American* article was blatant flattery. But Chan and Sengupta were more interested in how the participants' attitudes would be influenced subliminally. They set out to determine whether or not participants would develop a subconscious positive association with the store, even though they saw the ad as obvious pandering. Further, they wondered if such an implicit reaction would be a better predictor of decisions to do business with the store down the road. Would they be more inclined to show up at the store and make a purchase at some point?

Flattery turned out to be a more powerful motivator than they had realized. The implicit attitudes toward the store prevailed; they were more positive than explicit attitudes. They also served as reliable predictors of how likely participants would make purchases in the future. So even though participants immediately saw through the ploy, dismissing the ads on an explicit level, Chan and Sengupta concluded that "the flattery was exerting an important effect outside their awareness."[10]

At the heart of this phenomenon is the simple fact that people enjoy feeling good about themselves. Our brains are fertile ground for compliments, and people who understand how and when to plant those compliments gain a psychological advantage over others.

The researchers then probed more deeply into the relative effects of flattery. They wanted to see to what extent participants' self-esteem at the moment affected their receptivity to insincere flattery. They asked participants to write about two things: (1) an aspect of their personality that they'd like to change and (2) a personality trait they valued. The outcome was predictable: Those who had an easier time finding fault with themselves were more susceptible to the subliminal influences of flattery than those who focused on their strengths.

So, if your source shows signs of insecurity or questionable self-esteem, add "boosting ego" to your mix of techniques to move the conversation in the direction you desire. In your case, try to make the flattery valid on both an explicit and an implicit level—that is, make the compliment as relevant and believable as you can.

Returning to our young HR professional, if the person interviewing her for the job used an ego-boosting strategy, here is how it could fit: He might observe that she is a little nervous around him—normal for a job interview—so he decides to use an ego-up strategy to make her feel more empowered to talk with him candidly. "You've given great answers to my questions," he says, "and your track record shows you have a wonderful grasp of the complexities of a position in HR." After that, he could pose the question of whether or not she ever deviated from company policy and she might hear it positively. She might assume he expects her to say yes and explain what happened as a sign that she exercised good judgment in a tough situation.

Deflating Ego

Done well, attacking a person's sense of self-worth enables you to move the person into a vulnerable emotional state and make him more compliant. It's often best used in conjunction with another technique that later makes him feel better. You use the desire to reconnect with you to get your information, and then you bring him out of his self-esteem slump.

Done poorly, you could easily alienate the individual if you've misjudged how far to go with that person. And you might get pummeled by crossing the line from ego deflation to insult.

Looking at the worst-case scenario first, I'm reminded of a study done in the mid-1990s that concluded, "Don't ever insult a Southern man." The essence of it is that men from the Southern United States (not all men, of course, but Southern men in general) have a "culture of honor" that compels them to take action when insulted.[11] The study involved a group of men from the North and a group of men from the South, with individuals in both groups having someone bump into them and call them an asshole. Not only did the researchers observe body language and hear verbal responses among the Southerners that indicated they were more bothered by the insult than the Northerners, but they also measured testosterone levels, which markedly elevated among the Southern men. So maybe think carefully about how to moderate your deflating-ego technique when you try it out on a Southern man.

Normally, what happens is that puncturing someone's ego affects his comfort level with social interaction. You have to manage carefully what happens after that to accomplish your goal of motivating the conversation in a manner that's productive. A 2007 experiment with young men and women at Florida State University and San Diego State University spotlights the immediate effect of damaging someone's ego, and illustrates how you lose someone's cooperation completely if you don't follow up with some action or remark to help him boomerang back to you.

The researchers set out to determine how the students would respond to being evaluated on their social skills. The 20 participants were given name tags and put into small, same-sex groups. They were supposed to learn the first names of the other three to five people in the group, and talk with them for 20 minutes. The researchers then took participants into separate rooms and asked them to pick two of the people in their group they'd like to work with.

But the evaluations were rigged. The researchers arbitrarily told some of the students that everyone wanted to work with them. They told others that nobody wanted to work with them. So some heard these exact words, "I have good news for you—everyone chose you as someone they'd like to work with." Others heard, "I hate to tell you this, but no one chose you as someone they wanted to work with."[12]

Then one of the members of the research team took each person aside and said that there was a reason why he or she could not move on to the next task—such as the groups were full—but not to worry, there was another opportunity to participate. Each one was told, "You can either leave now and get the hour credit for the experiment, or if you think you can help out me and the other experimenters, you can do some other experiments for us—each takes about 15 minutes and you could do one, two, or three. Doing the other experiments won't affect the amount of credit you get. What you do is up to you."[13]

Participants who thought they'd been rejected by their peers volunteered for far fewer experiments than those who'd been accepted. The difference in cooperation was remarkable: Whereas 90 percent of the accepted participants volunteered, only 20 percent of the rejected ones said they would help.

The team doing the experiment thought they might see more of the rejected participants willing to come back and help because they would want to generate some kind of favorable response to their contribution. Not so. Whether they resented what happened, or just had such a profound sense of embarrassment over being rejected, most of the rejected participants walked out.

Watch the body language of someone you use a deflating-ego technique with. If you see the person close up—arms folded in front as though she's hugging herself, slight slump of shoulders, head down—you know you've succeeded in undermining her sense of self-worth. At that point, give her an immediate path to reconnect by providing you information, and then go back to your rapport-building techniques.

In contrast, the researchers simply asked the rejected students to perform a task; there was no psychological or emotional reward associated with doing it.

Putting the deflating-ego technique in the context of a real situation will show that it doesn't have to be nearly as harsh as "no one chose you as someone they wanted to work with." For example, if the person interviewing the young woman for the HR position suggested that her minimal experience in the field might be a problem in the new job, she would likely feel uneasy and want to prove herself. Again, his aim is to find out if she has deviated from company policies in the past, so he might say, "Our company prides itself on intelligent, and even customized, handling of human resource issues. We are very tuned into our employees' needs. I'm sorry to say that I'm concerned you just don't have the breadth of experience yet to make those mature choices." In this instance, she feels she can prove him wrong by citing instances when she deviated from policy in the interest of employee morale or to help someone avert a personal crisis. Even just a nod or other look of approval from the interviewer might give her the validation she seeks and put her at ease once again.

Easing Fears

Eric Maddox, the distinguished Army Sergeant whose interrogation and analysis led to the capture of Saddam Hussein, contributed many insights for this book, and they are primarily featured in Chapter 9. He has several stories in his book *Mission: Black List #1* that illustrate his use of an easing-fears approach; this one places us toward the end of Maddox's journey—having interviewed more than 300 people—to extract the truth that would lead him to Saddam Hussein. At this point, he is facing Muhammad Khudayr, the person who can take him to Muhammad Ibrahim, leader of the insurgency and the direct link to the former dictator.

> At the beginning of the interrogation, the prisoner had denied even knowing Muhammad Ibrahim. Now he was telling me how afraid he was of the man. His fear was well founded. If it were discovered that he was cooperating with us, his life and the life of his family

would be in jeopardy. I needed to find a way to help him with that problem.

"I tell you what," I offered. "You take me to Muhammad Ibrahim and I'll make sure that everyone knows that Muslit, his son, was the one that helped capture him. He's scheduled to be shipped off to Guantánamo Bay in a few days. Once he's gone, we can blame it all on him. You'll be in the clear."[14]

Maddox eased the fears of Muhammad Khudayr, who succumbed to the seduction of being protected. Maddox watched his body language—face sagging and shoulders slumped—and realized that the ploy had worked. It was a ploy he described as "pure bullshit,"[15] but it worked.

Mitigating or removing the fear of someone that you want to confide in you is one of the most powerful tools in your arsenal of conversation motivators. Gregory Hartley, my co-author on *How to Spot a Liar*, told a personal story to illustrate the technique in the first edition of that book. He rear-ended a woman's sedan with his one-ton pickup truck and crushed the trunk region of her car. She jumped out crying and screaming. He hugged her and apologized, a combination of actions that calmed her down immediately. She was far less inclined to run to a lawyer, and far more inclined to share with him that it was really some other stress at home that made her react so wildly rather than the car accident.

Physicians in fields such as oncology and cardiology commonly face patients who have tremendous anxiety about a diagnosis or the outcome of a proposed procedure. They need the conversational tool of easing fear to get the patients to talk openly about how they feel, lifestyle issues that might impede treatment, and so on, in order to help them. There are also many possible situations at a workplace where someone's competence or honesty comes into question, and the prospect of being fired makes him close up and not want to divulge anything about himself or others out of fear.

Offer protection—emotional, psychological, and, if necessary, physical—to help boost the person's feeling of security and trust in you, and then carry on with the conversation.

Certainty/Uncertainty

Projecting certainty about what you know can another person to talk openly. This is the value of doing your homework about your source: You can go into a conversation with a level of detail on at least a few issues that suggest you know more about the person than you do. This is often how Hanns Scharff got his prisoners to talk about military capabilities. He convinced them he already had the information, so they felt there was no reason to hold back in conversation.

Immediately before Eric Maddox's encounter with Muhammad Khudayr, described previously, Maddox used certainty, or we-know-all in military terms, to move his prisoner to acknowledge that he knew the target, Muhammad Ibrahim, and his whereabouts. He told his prisoner: "I know you are lying to me because you think I am unsure of my information. But you are wrong. I know everything about you. I know all the crimes you have committed. And I know that the only way you can escape punishment is to take me to Muhammad Ibrahim."[16]

The ploy worked, with Muhammad Khudayr immediately protesting that if he took Maddox to Muhammad Ibrahim, he would be killed. Maddox then closed the deal by using his easing fears approach to assure him that wouldn't happen.

Uncertainty on the part of the source can also help you motivate the conversation. A person feels a little off balance and out of control in the face of uncertainty. Jim McCormick, author of *The Power of Risk,* has done research about how to mitigate uncertainty; he suggests turning what he tells his audiences and readers upside down in order to engender it: "If the person perceives that he's facing a greater risk than he can handle, the level of uncertainty will escalate. It could be any kind of risk: physical, career, financial, social, intellectual, creative, emotional, or spiritual. At that point, the person's rising emotions make him less able to make well-reasoned choices."[17]

If your source is in that state of mild confusion—not completely disoriented, but a little off balance—the information you're after may leak out because the person has less control over what he says. In addition, if you project certainty while asking your questions, you potentially get cooperation; you're pulling the person toward more solid ground.

Silence

Japanese call it *shiin.* It's that awkward silence in a conversation that causes people to glance at their laptops, shift their posture, and look at the door as though they hope someone will enter the room and end the tension. Finally, someone can't tolerate it any longer and says something, anything.

Michael Handford, a professor of linguistics and international communications consultant, has researched how cultural orientation affects how soon we reach the point where we hope someone breaks the silence. Spanish speakers have the lowest tolerance, at just a second or two. English speakers are up to three or four seconds. Japanese speakers have a rather high tolerance at five or six seconds.[18] The foundation for his conclusions is records of about a million words of business meetings. More than 25 companies in England, Germany, Ireland, and Japan allowed him to bring his microphone into their meetings to collect the data.

A first consideration in using silence as a conversation motivator, then, is to have some basic sense of your source's tolerance for a conversation lull.

Creating silence in the modern world is intentional. Even in a room full of people experiencing *shiin,* anyone has the option of speaking up, even if it's just to beg, "Will somebody please say something!" To many people, if not most, silence is unsettling, and someone *will* say something; it may even contain some substance.

The modern human's aversion to silence can be so strong that it arouses fear. When there is no tapping on a keyboard, no humming of an air conditioner, no traffic noise in the distance, people can feel alienated from their environment. Drawing on six years of research involving 580 undergraduate students, Bruce Fell of Charles Sturt University in Australia concluded that they had a "need for noise and their struggle with silence is learnt behaviour."[19]

The military tactic of using silence as an approach is for the interrogator to remain silent, perhaps while maintaining penetrating eye contact. Ideally, the source feels uncomfortable or even fearful, and starts blurting out things to establish or restore some kind of connection. Outside of that context, using silence would look at lot different unless you are grilling a suspect. Either maintaining a stare or turning away, so that your body becomes a barrier, indicates hostility, disgust, or some other negative response. That effect wouldn't work well if you're a therapist or social worker trying to get your client to tell you the dark secrets of her horrible childhood.

You would have to remain silent while projecting the message through your body language that you want the person to speak.

To get a little more sophisticated about using silence as a conversation motivator, consider that silence in a conversation can be much more than the absence of speech. How you introduce the silence can have huge significance. Composer John Cage has a famous piece called *4'33"*, meaning four minutes and 33 seconds. By my watching, at two minutes and 44 seconds after coming on stage, he lifts his baton.[20] The orchestra has some movement of pages and lifting of instruments. Tension mounts in the audience, with some nervous coughs interrupting the silence. Cage turns a page and wipes his brow. He resumes an almost Buddha-like posture and then lifts his baton again. The camera moves to a page in a bassoon player's sheet music. It says, "Movement 2—Tacet," which indicates that the instrument is silent. More nervous coughs erupt in the audience. Cage is watching a clock on his podium with the seconds ticking away. At precisely the right moment—he turns a page and all of the musicians shuffle, scratch their jaws, or stroke their instruments. And then, four minutes and 33 seconds after the performance began, John Cage leaves the stage and the audience erupts with wild applause.

John Cage introduced silence as a musical experience. *4'33"* has been something that arouses fascination, passion (positive and negative), appreciation, and curiosity among those who have performed it and "heard" it since it premiered in 1952.

The range of applications that silence can have as a motivator of verbal and non-verbal response is expansive. There is the military interrogator's silent approach as a technique of intimidation on one end. And then on the other, there are conversational equivalents of Cage's provocative and inviting use of silence, such as the relaxed way a college professor might pose a complex question and then wait patiently until a student formulates an answer. Silence can also frame an experience to get people thinking about what they just said and what they are about to say. This is a common experience in religious rituals like the Catholic Mass.

Choosing Your Motivators

The Army Field Manual containing the approaches described earlier reads, "With the exception of the direct approach, no other approach is effective by itself. Interrogators use different approach techniques or combine them into a cohesive, logical technique...the combinations are unlimited."[21]

The way Eric Maddox combined the use of certainty with easing his prisoner's fears efficiently drove his source toward answers. Maddox was running out of time because he was about to be transferred, so he had to choose his approaches carefully to get the job done quickly.

If you're a person who is "paid to be charming," like Peter Earnest or Jack Devine, motivators might take the conversation in a more circuitous path, with incentives such as *quid pro quo* and ego-boosting comments used to establish a trusting, and even friendly, relationship.

Fundamental to choosing what techniques you use is how comfortable you are with them. Some people could never use a deflating ego approach without feeling mean; others would get so nervous trying to use silence that their fidgeting would ruin the effect. Do what's natural for you and for the circumstance. Pay attention to the person from whom you want information and get your cues on your next move from what she says and what her body language tells you about her emotional state.

Remember not only to say the right thing in the right place, but far more difficult still, to leave unsaid the wrong thing at the tempting moment.

—Benjamin Franklin

In every interview, negotiation, or investigation, when you are after information for a purpose, you need to manage the conversation. In general, it won't be advantageous for your control over the direction to be obvious to the other person, though; the guidance in this chapter helps you do it subtly.

Begin by giving your source credit for having the ability to navigate a conversation, even if she's a 19-year-old applying for her first full-time job. Approach the situation as though you are playing chess: You begin the game with the same number of pieces, all of which have the same capability. The difference is that you've carefully considered your strategy on using them, whereas she probably hasn't.

This chapter covers the four main tools of managing a conversation: analytic listening, directed questioning, choosing the location, and knowing how to play the Kevin Bacon game.

Analytic Listening

Listening means paying attention to what someone is saying. I think of analytic listening as paying attention with a specific purpose, and it has three interrelated elements: keywords, an open mind, and synchronous pacing.

Keywords

Your source's use of keywords and concepts can indicate whether or not you are on a conversational path to getting the information you need. Sometimes you need to plant those words and concepts into the conversation if they have dropped out or have been missing altogether, or you will find yourself having a dialogue about something irrelevant.

For example, in a January 21, 2014 interview on NPR's *Fresh Air,* host Terry Gross interviewed Joaquin Phoenix, who had just been nominated for an Academy Award for his performance in the movie *Her.* He was an engaging guest who seemed sincerely interested in giving a good interview—he gives very few—but he would occasionally wander off the trail. During his biggest diversion, he made a series of comments about how boring he was, ending with: "Sometimes I just, you know, I just think, who cares?" Gross replied: "We, who love movies, care."[1] With that she looped him right back to the point of the conversation—that is, Joaquin Phoenix's movies.

One of my friends in the intelligence community, whom I'll call Jack, told me a story that illustrates how much you can learn about someone by tuning in to keywords—and that includes noticing that keywords are missing from a conversation. Jack decided to get a personal trainer. At the second session, during the 10-minute warmup portion of the workout, Jack asked the trainer what she does for fun. She told him that she has a new boyfriend and they go fishing together. For the remaining nine minutes of Jack's warm-up on the recumbent bike, she told him about hooks with no barbs, the challenges of casting well, what time of day to use different lures for different fish, and how fish at different locations require different lures. Jack thought all of this was intriguing, but not because he found the information fascinating. Not once did he hear the word "fun" come back to him. Not once did she describe what it was like to catch a fish. He speculated that she didn't care about fishing; perhaps she liked the science of fishing and the process of fishing, but not actually catching fish. Or, maybe what she really liked was having the boyfriend share his knowledge and excitement with her about his favorite activity. He stored that thought and decided to follow up on it the following week.

Monday morning, he came into the gym and went straight to the bike to warm up. His trainer offered him a "good morning," after which he said, "It was a gorgeous weekend. Did you and your boyfriend go fishing?" She said, "Well," and then there was a long pause followed by, "My boyfriend went fishing, but I decided to catch up on some paperwork." She didn't join the boyfriend where he was fishing until later in the day when a people started to gather for an evening barbeque.

The following Monday morning was a repeat of the previous Monday's conversation, with the only difference being "housework" instead of paperwork, which she had to do because her mom was coming for a visit. He knew the mom wasn't arriving for two weeks.

During the next few weeks, Jack heard nothing more about fishing. A few weeks later, he heard nothing more about the boyfriend. He had already told me the first part of the story and was ready to put money on the fact that the trainer was not going to go the distance with the guy who loved fishing. Among other things, the keywords were missing.

An Open Mind

If your internal voice is responding to the person with mockery or boredom, then you are more engaged in judging than listening. Control those thought balloons rising above your head; your source might sense they are there. It's important to allow yourself to doubt, but don't cross the line into cynicism or criticism.

To put it in media terms, you don't want to be like an advocacy journalist. A common occurrence in advocacy journalism is for the host of a program to air emotionally charged opinions while asking a guest a question. The result is often tension, not answers. Bill O'Reilly is a political commentator and the host of the television show *The O'Reilly Factor* who confronted Congressman Barney Frank about his role in the U.S. portion of the global financial crisis of 2008. Frank, a politician who had served 32 years in the House of Representatives before his retirement in 2013, was chairman of the House Financial Services Committee at the time. O'Reilly began his interview with the question "Shouldn't everybody in the country be angry with you right now?"[2] Frank stuck to his facts and talking points, and answered the question, but that's probably not what people who tuned in remember from the interview. They remember challenges like O'Reilly's next question: "That's swell, but you still went out in July and said that everything was great and, off that, a lot of people bought stock and lost everything they had." After that, it seemed highly improbable that discerning viewers would get actual information from the exchange.

Synchronous Pacing

Many of us who are fast-talkers have a tendency to finish other people's sentences if their pace is slower than ours. If you want to get the most out of your listening, do not step on someone else's sentences, either by trying to finish them or by interrupting to interject a thought. Your pursuit of information will stop short when you do this.

In the early days of my writing career, I had the opportunity to interview an Olympic gold medalist in a slalom event to get her insights about both mental and physical training. We connected like we were old friends. Unfortunately, that made me too comfortable in taking the conversation into a more personal discussion of training, and I lost sight of the big picture—what she could tell my readers about *their* training. I stepped on her words, took her down a different path, and nearly lost those insights forever.

Directed Questioning

Directed questioning is the use of questions to steer a conversation. Differentiating among types of questions is a valuable starting point, because asking what we might term "bad" questions will often cause you to lose control of the exchange.

James O. Pyle, my co-author of *Find Out Anything From Anyone, Anytime,* sorts questions into six good and four bad types. The "bad" questions can have value when they are used deliberately, but the problem is that most of us use them without any planning, so they tend to derail a conversation.

The good questions are:

1. **Direct:** This is a straightforward question that opens with a basic interrogative word or phrase. You begin with *who, what, when where, why,* or *how* to get a narrative response, and something like *did you, do you, would you,* or *could you* to get a yes or no.

2. **Control:** You know the answer to a control question when you ask it. It helps you detect a lie, figure out if the person is uninformed, or confirm that he's paying attention. For

example, your manager might ask, "Were you able to get that report to James in time for his 10 o'clock meeting?" She knows you were not, but she wants to know if you will be honest about the problem.

3. **Repeat:** Pyle's definition, and the one he teaches, is one of two variations. The Army Field Manual suggests that one way to handle a repeat question is to ask the same question as part of a mechanism to wear down the source. In contrast, Pyle instructs that they are two or more different questions related to the same information and that they reinforce each other. This distinction is very useful in dealing with someone who may have misunderstood, misheard, or wished to avoid the question the first time it was posed. One example is the anesthesiologist asking you the morning of your surgery, "When was the last time you had anything to eat or drink?" Aware that you were supposed to have nothing after midnight, you might say, "Midnight." Toward the end of the conversation, the same doctor might say, "It's 8 o'clock now and we're ready to get you prepped for surgery. You must be thirsty by now. How long has it been since you've anything to drink?" Your mind goes back to that water you had sometime early this morning and you say, "About four hours."

4. **Follow-Up:** Also known as a "persistent question," this is the same question either reshaped a little or simply repeated to explore different angles of the desired information. A version of a follow-up question is simply "What else?" So, a therapist might ask her client, "Do you do anything to try to alleviate your depression?" The client replies, "I go for walks." The therapist suspects the client may also be self-medicating, so she asks, "What else do you do?"

5. **Summary:** The question allows the source to revisit an answer. You're feeding back information, perhaps repeating word for word something the person has said. For example, a mom might say to her son, "Do I understand you correctly that there were three other boys involved in the fight?" Just be careful and don't turn this into a compound question by trying to consolidate information. An example of this mistake is: "Do I understand you correctly that there were three other boys involved in the fight and six girls were standing around watching?"

6. **Non-Pertinent:** Although it's called a non-pertinent question because it ostensibly does not relate to the information you're seeking, it can be extremely useful in getting a nervous person to talk or in establishing rapport with someone, even a hostile source. In a job interview, it might be a question about the traffic the candidate encountered on the way to appointment. On a first date, it might be "What do you think of all this rain?" If the response is a grouchy "It sucks!" then the question may actually be a pertinent one in terms of your dating future.

The following four types of questions are considered bad because they lose the aspect of good questioning that supports the discovery of information. They involve assumptions, confuse information, and lose information.

1. **Leading:** Your question supplies an answer. The police officer who collars a disheveled young man outside a building is asking a leading question when he says, "You were in the building when the fight started, weren't you?" The officer has no proof, but if he gets a yes out of the young man, then he has a suspect.

2. **Negative:** Using negative words like *never* and *not* can corrupt the intended meaning of the question. A typical abuse is "Are you not okay?" I've often heard people say, "Yes" in response—meaning, "Yes, I'm okay," even though that's what not the questioner asked.

3. **Vague:** This type of question lacks clarity, so the source may not be sure what information is being requested. Example: "When you heard all the noise and walked down the street past those trucks, what did you see was going on?" It's unclear if the question relates to what was going on where the noise was, or maybe what was going on with the trucks. When you ask a vague question, if the source intends to hide the facts from you, this sets him up to hide them without even lying to you.

4. **Compound:** A compound question poses two or more questions at one time. This is a common shortcoming of journalists who feel they have limited time with a source such as the president of the United States. In the December 20, 2013 press conference with President Obama, one of the White House correspondents asked the true value of the National Security Agency's (NSA) bulk metadata, such as that at the center of the Edward Snowden controversy. The reporter asked the president both to identify examples of its usefulness and give his opinion on two things: the usefulness of the data, and whether or not the NSA should continue to its data collection practices. Certainly, the questions are related, but they are best expressed separately. Putting them together gives the source an easy out to answer one of the questions and slide past the other.

In addition to using each type of question with intention, selecting your conversation motivators well supports your taking a conversation in the direction you want. Whether it's using an incentive like a *quid pro quo* exchange of personal information or an ego-boosting remark, you can keep a person engaged in the topic you want her to be engaged in.

Regardless of how skillfully you handle questioning, sometimes people want to go in a direction that is not consistent with what you have in mind; you don't think that direction will get you the information you need. You face three options:

▶ Acknowledge what the person is talking about, but move her back to the subject you want to discuss. One way to do this is to feign interest: "That's something I'd enjoying talking with you about, but before we move on, tell me more about..."

▶ Tune in to why the person shifted topics. Your source might be giving you even more valued information that you'd been getting before. You hear keywords that pertain to your area of peak interest and might think, "Wow! Glad he's headed down this path."

▶ Go with the flow. If you have the time and patience, you could let the person keep talking about the new subject to find out if there is an important point or piece of information that will surface. Many people love to wrap their insights and information in stories. They start telling you about their dog when you were sharing your anxiety over a dental appointment. It might be five minutes before it's clear that the dog story has a direct connection to your concerns about your dental appointment.

The following dialogue is an example of elicitation conducted by Jim Pyle over the telephone. Elicitation can involve directed questioning, but fundamentally it's a conversation designed to get a source to talk to you in a focused way without divulging your true intent. This brief exchange illustrates how someone skilled in elicitation techniques gets a simple piece of information *without* coming out and asking for it directly.

Jim: So you're writing a book, huh?

Source: Yes, and I appreciate your taking the time to talk with me about it.

Jim: Certainly. So where are you located?

Source: Estes Park, Colorado.

Jim: I'm back East, sitting on a deck chair, enjoying the cool evening breezes. But I'm thinking that, this time of day where you are, the sun is still high in the sky.

Source: We have blue skies and mountains all around us!

Jim: Where we are, the trees go up about 80 feet into the sky, so we lose the sun a little earlier than some folks around us. It's really cooling off right now. But you must be used to cool temperatures in the summer being in the mountains.

Source: It's been unusually hot here lately.

Jim: Really?

Source: Usually people come to Estes Park because it's mid-70s in the summertime. But it was 90 degrees today and I'd say that's been going on for three days.

Jim: I heard about some big cool wave coming out of Canada and thought you would have been swept up in that cold weather.

Source: Nope. It's been hot.

Pyle's aim was to find out the recent temperatures in that part of Colorado. The point was never to ask the question directly, but to get the information through directed questioning. Non-pertinent questions have an important role in this exercise—and keep this in mind when you review Eric Maddox's interrogation system in Chapter 9.

This basic technique just demonstrated is also how you would question someone about a sensitive issue or about something she wants to hide. Here is how this might play out in an interview if you paired a skilled questioner with a guarded celebrity. In this case, it's a journalist who wants to know the story behind why this celebrity has never had children. He sets up a couple of avenues in his mind about how he could get to the topic without offending her, because she has shut down more than one interview when asked direct questions of a personal nature. The basis for this is an actual interview that has been changed to protect both the interviewer and the interviewee.

Howard: I've read a lot about you. You've had a wonderful and intriguing life, but are you like me? Do you ever ask yourself: What could I have done differently?

Source: Oh, that's such a great question. [*This is a phrase that people insert to buy themselves time. The question has caused them to pause and try to calculate an answer.*]

Source: Hmmmm. I think if there was one thing I would have done differently, it was to indulge myself intellectually in more study of science. I went headlong into theater. And I loved the theater, but—and this is a terrible thing to admit—I wasn't necessarily enamored with theater people. There were many people I liked, but there were many people who were extremely insecure. But I hung out—and this is not only in college, but also after I started working in professional theater—with lots of scientists. I even dated a professor in chemistry. A lot of my best friends were in science.

Howard: Science is a big field. What kind of science interested you most?

Source: People science. Science of the brain. It's the science that explains human behavior which is part of why I was drawn to theater—to understand people. I think it would have been a good thing for me to get the academic credentials in that field.

Howard: What about your human behavior would you have studied?

Source: What?

Howard: What would you have studied to give you some personal benefit? After all, isn't that why any of us goes headlong into anything?

Source: Ah. Yes. Hmmm. I think maybe my yin/yang relationship with risk. I am incredibly prone to take certain types of risks, but at the same time, there are other types of risks I completely back off from. There were wild things I did physically and in my career that people thought were crazy, but there were other things, like motherhood, that I thought, "I'm never going there." [Laughing] That's way too big a risk.

Howard: Too big a risk?

Source: Way too big a risk. I'm never going there.

Howard: How close did you get—you know, to even thinking about it?

Source: Pretty close. I mean, I was married.

Howard: Marriage is a relationship. But motherhood is an experience. How close did you get to that experience?

> [*At this point, there is momentary silence. But Howard does not try to break it. He knows that she will either continue the conversation and he will get what he wants, or she will end it right here.*]

Source: Um. Close enough.

Howard: A lot of people, given that opportunity, make choices.

Source: Or your body makes choices for you.

Howard: True, but people also make choices for the body.

Source: That's very true.

Howard: A lot of that happens in the world today and it polarizes people.

Source: It sure does. Like look at what's going on in Massachusetts.

Howard: What's going on there?

Source: The Supreme Court struck down a Massachusetts law requiring protestors to stay away from the entrance to abortion clinics. So a couple of weeks later—and this is, like, record time—Massachusetts passed a law to help those women who want an abortion to get their rights back and not have to deal with the harassment.

> [*Any questioner at this point would detect not only the emotion of the response, but also keywords such as "rights" that indicate the source's point of view.*]

Howard: You have great empathy for these women.

Source: Of course!

Howard: Wow. You may not have studied the science of
         the brain, but you certainly have insights into how
         people think and feel in a tough situation. This is
         sure one of them. I know a lot of people who don't
         have children either by default or by choice.

Source: I made a choice.

In an exchange like this, it's critical to follow source leads. A
source lead is information dropped by the source in the course
of conversation that you feel there is value in pursuing—that is,
an additional person, place, thing, or event may be mentioned
that warrants attention.

Directed questioning can also involve volunteering certain
information to pull the source down a path of your design. Law
enforcement professionals use this all the time with suspects.
They offer one fact in a case—something they know to be true
and that the suspect knows to be true—and then wait for the
suspect to add something to it. For example, a detective might
start by saying, "The victim had a wound in the upper part of
the body." The suspect might come back with, "I didn't shoot
her!" First, the detective never said anything about shooting;
second, he never said anything about the gender of the victim.

Good journalists are highly skilled in all aspects of directed
questioning. It's not an accident that they can take someone
who is accustomed to being dogmatic and lead him into delivering a worthwhile interview. For example, Richard Sakwa is
an opinionated man who harshly criticizes certain Western
policies and actions in relation to Russia. Author of *Putin and
the Oligarchs,* Sakwa is a professor of Russian and European
politics and head of the School of International Relations at
the University of Kent. Interviewing him would be a tough
challenge for just about anyone in broadcasting in the United

States and many European nations because Sakwa holds a number of views that are unpopular in those countries. The tendency might be to push back, which could have two negative outcomes: infuse the interview with too much emotion, and prevent Sakwa from delivering generous doses of important information. As with any interviewee who has an agenda—that is, he wants to air particular ideas and knows how to maneuver a conversation to do so—Sakwa is the kind of guest who tests a broadcast journalist's ability to control the conversation.

After listening to Jeremy Hobson's interview with Richard Sakwa on NPR's *Here and Now,* I sent Hobson a note about it because, in critical ways, it seemed masterful to me. He asked yes-or-no questions to illuminate Sakwa's points of view, followed by "why" questions to allow his guest to explain his views with stories from history and current events. My note to Hobson asked if it had gone the way he wanted because that's the determinant of whether or not a person controls a conversation. His reply noted, "There were a lot of things he said that I wanted to challenge—and I did challenge some of them— but I didn't want to veer off the path of the interview. I didn't have enough time to go down all the rabbit holes with him, so I picked my battles to keep us on track."[3]

In my interview with Hobson,[4] I asked him to specify the techniques he uses to steer an on-air conversation. They apply to someone in any profession:

▶ Huge emphasis on homework. He wants to be prepared to ask not only the questions, but also the follow-up questions. This was what he did with Sakwa: He first clarified Sakwa's position on key issues and then followed up with specific "why" questions.

▶ Relying on "what do you mean" questions to give a guest the change to provide a clearer explanation of a point of view or concept.

▶ Repeating a question in a different form when the guest is evasive about answering. He finds this particularly useful with politicians who like to hedge on certain issues: "Even though I don't get an answer, I show they aren't giving me an answer."

▶ Opening a question with some version of "yes or no," and then posing the question to increase the chances of getting a definite answer on a position. For example, in an interview with one guest about recent border incidents, he asked, "Yes or no: do you think they should be deported?" and the guest finally responded, "I'm not going to give you a yes or no." That answer revealed a great deal about the guest, who was an outspoken opponent to immigration reform and had stated previously he was in favor of people being deported.

Choosing the Venue

Choosing the location for your conversation can provide distinct advantages. There are two ways to approach the issue of location:

1. Take the other person out of her physical comfort zone and put her into your space so that it's most likely easier for you to project and maintain control.

2. Choose a location that affords security and privacy so the person will feel inclined to speak freely.

Many Catholic confessionals combine both: relatively small, dimly lit sets of two or three connected rooms, each just a bit larger than an old-fashioned phone booth. The person confessing sins sits or kneels on one side of a partition, and the priest sits in the darkness on the other side. Most people are out of their comfort zone because of the darkness, the constrained space, the awkward position, and the fact that there is an expectation that they will be telling their transgressions. They are also in a blessed place—namely, what they see as the House of the Lord—so there is an intimidation factor. At the same time, the environment affords tremendous privacy, at least while you're inside. In whispers, you tell the priest all the horrible things you've done—every one of them since the last time you went to Confession.

In normal life, you probably won't come close to a confessional type of experience, but the elements of the setup give useful clues about what gets people to spill their guts.

There is another factor at play here that can be useful in determining the location of the exchange you will have with your source: ritual. In the confessional, the person who has come seeking forgiveness says certain things to the priest, and the priest says certain things to the individual. Ritual runs throughout the experience, even down to what the priest wears to perform his role in the sacrament.

A venue like the boss's office can trigger ritualistic behavior. The person coming to see the boss will often sit on the opposite side of desk in a deferential manner. If that employee's goal is to get information from the boss about the possibility of a raise and promotion, that venue will not support her goal. She might ask if they could meet for coffee at the company cafeteria at a time when there is minimal traffic and people who work there always greet her by name.

Consider your source's level of rigidity about his environment when choosing location. One of my friends worked with a lobbyist in Washington, D.C., who was a creature of habit unlike anyone else she had ever met: medium starch on the shirts, office with knickknacks in precisely the same location in all of the three offices he occupied while they worked together, replacing his car with the same model every other year, arriving and departing work at the same time every day. She told me he was in a prime position to help her make a career move to Capitol Hill, but she needed to find out up-front if he would even be willing to do it. What should she do?

I knew he was a news junkie. I suggested that she work a little later one day to match his schedule and invite him to watch a particular news show with her before they both left for the day. He agreed, and while they were in the conference room with the television on, she broached the subject of helping her out. He was sitting on a leather couch—not his usual desk chair—and seemed less rigid in this environment than usual. He said, "Of course. Let's have lunch on Friday and talk more about this."

It's possible that he would have agreed if she'd asked him while sitting on the other side of his gigantic desk in his office. But the fact is, she had more control over the interaction because she chose a more relaxing setting; it worked for both of them.

Four, Five, or Six Degrees of Separation

Playing the Kevin Bacon game means making connections between seemingly unrelated topics or facts so that you steer the conversation where you want it to go. It's a variation of six degrees of separation, based on the mathematical premise that, by association, everyone on earth is only six people away from everyone else. In the Kevin Bacon game, it's figuring out how Actor X connects with actor Kevin Bacon—with the point being that you always come back to Kevin Bacon. If you are skilled at making connections, you can always find a way back to the topic you really want to address in a conversation.

For example, say a rumor about massive layoffs has been flying up and down the hallways at your office. You've heard that thousands of people might lose their jobs, and you want to find out if you might be one of them. Vanessa, your regional HR director, is a tight-lipped individual; nothing confidential or inappropriate ever seems to leak out of her mouth. But Vanessa is the one person in the building who would know if there was going to be layoffs. You knock on her door and ask to see her for a couple of minutes.

Vanessa: Sure, come in.

You: Wanted to get a quick opinion. I thought I'd take a week of my leave and go to the Dodgers' adult baseball camp.

Vanessa: Sounds like fun. My opinion is "Go for it!"

You: Yeah, but I also thought I could spend the time in a course to get ready to take the exam to get my certification in personal training.

Vanessa: That's interesting. Are you thinking of switching careers?

You: Not anytime soon, but I was thinking that a good post-retirement option might be that I could work as a trainer.

Vanessa: Wow—that's some good long-term planning considering your age. But it sounds like this is a passion for you. Are you happy with what you're doing now?

You: As long as the company continues to support all the skills upgrades I need to stay current, I'm very happy.

Vanessa: Well, you know the company has had to cut back
         in a lot of areas, and training just might be one of
         them.

You: Really?

Vanessa: The company has a lot of cost-reduction measures
         that are probably going into effect soon.

You: Like what?

At this point, you've probably heard all you need to hear from Vanessa. The last two comments she made involved the phrases "cut back" and "cost-reduction measures." She also insulated herself from the concepts—in effect, putting a barrier between her and the bad news—by starting her sentence with "the company." Without telling you about layoffs, she's leaking what's on her mind *and* how she feels about it. To conclude, you let her know that she's helped a lot and that you've decided to take the course in preparation for the certification exam. When she gives you a broad smile and says, "I think that's a great choice," you have additional confirmation of the layoff. She won't be as stressed out about giving you a pink slip if you're on your way to another career.

The skill of making connections between one topic and another to get the information you need is probably something you do every day and don't even realize it. When you have an agenda, all you need to do is find a seamless way to connect what you need to know with whatever someone is saying. The operative word is "seamless."

Exercise: Connecting Concepts to Manage a Conversation

Take two topics that seem to have no relationship and see how you can move smoothly from one to the other. To illustrate how this might happen, I randomly chose two unrelated headlines from MSN.com on July 23, 2014: "McDonald's Fires Mom who Let Girl Play Alone" and "Mars to Raise Chocolate Prices."

Person 1: What do you think of McDonald's firing this single mom who let her daughter play in a park nearby while she was working her shift?

Person 2: It's complicated, but my gut reaction is that mom was doing what she had to do and the kid had lots of other adults watching over her.

Person 1: I agree. I feel bad for the mom, not only because of the police arresting her, but also the backlash from righteous people. I mean, people in her position can't afford to have nannies watching their kids every minute!

Person 2: So true. We are in such stressful economic times— and I mean most of us who aren't rich—that I can see this happening with lots of well-intentioned parents.

Person 1: This problem, what this mom is dealing with, is part of a much bigger issue. We just have a lot of gigantic economic problems that make it hard to be good parents, run a small business—you name it.

Person 2: No kidding! My neighbor has a chocolate shop in town and she told me that the cost of cocoa has gone up more than 50 percent this year, so her chocolate suppliers are killing her!

Person 1: Yeah, I read that Hershey, Mars, and Nestle are all raising the prices of their chocolate candy.

Here is your challenge: Take two topics on a page of news and link them within six steps. It doesn't matter if it's a newspaper, MSN.com, or any other news source. It won't matter if it's fighting in Gaza and 401(K) retirement plans in the United States, or Justin Bieber and ragweed, you can find a way to get from one subject to the other without the process being laborious.

Listening in concert with questioning well helps you avoid the pitfalls that prevent you from getting the truth—or at least keeping yourself on the path toward it. The pitfalls include missing clues like keywords that tell you what the person knows and is focused on, misdirecting a conversation by asking a bad question, and talking too much. This last pitfall may be the biggest mistake that people in need of information often make in a sales situation, negotiation, interview, or even a personal conversation.

The discipline, the culture of how you approach information is what's important.[1]

—Jack Devine,
author, *Good Hunting: An American Spymaster's Story,* former head of CIA operations outside the United States

Truth gives you a critical sense of direction and focus; a deep and meaningful understanding of reality.[2]

—Ray Decker,
former GAO director, Combating Terrorism Assessments, and retired intelligence officer

Enter the search "Why didn't we stop 9/11?" into a search engine and you will probably get what I got: more than 22 million results. At the top of the list is an April 17, 2004 satirical piece by Pulitzer Prize–winning journalist Nicholas Kristof in the *New York Times*. Kristof imagines a conversation between a CIA briefer and President George W. Bush, who utters "Gosh" and "Whoa" when hearing about intelligence related to Osama bin Laden. Although the make-believe exchange suggests that the data points had come together to create a picture of exactly how bin Laden was going to attack, Kristof is careful to note that "[s]uch an imagined conversation is a bit unfair because it has the clarity of hindsight."[3]

Unfortunately, many other discussions about the subject weren't launched by rational people like Kristof. In article after article, you see attacks on America's failure to analyze the available data—the supposed intelligence malfunction that's now widely referred to as a "failure to connect the dots." One April 26, 2008 article—"9/11 Was Foreseeable"—lists various pieces of evidence to support the assertion of the title.[4] And who does the article say was to blame? It's a very impressive list that includes the FBI, National Intelligence Council, CIA, Federal Aviation Administration, Department of Justice, NSA, Pentagon officials, and North American Aerospace Defense Command (NORAD). Even author Salman Rushdie suppos- edly had a heads-up that something might happen. Hyperlinks litter the page, so I decided to find out where they went.

My following of the links yielded this sampling of results, many of which were plagued by link rot:

▶ The source of the Salman Rushie evidence involved a dead link.

▶ The source of the assertion that Condoleezza Rice was warned on September 6, 2001, that a terrorist attack inside the United States was imminent was Senator Gary Hart, who had just given a speech on terrorism and made an appointment with Rice to share his concerns.

▶ The source that U.S. officials had received warn- ing in 1998 of a "bin Laden plot involving aircraft in new York and Washington" involved a link to

CNN's home page. A search of the quoted phrase on the CNN site leads to a news-analysis piece by a CNN columnist.

▶ The source of a report to U.S. officials—a report of unnamed origin—that "a group of unidentified Arabs planned to fly an explosive-laden plane... into the World Trade Center" ["..." suggesting missing text is included in the article] also involved a dead link.

There are three interrelated points to be made here about data analysis:

1. Check your sources before you contend you have evidence.

2. Use your imagination but remove your biases when you analyze information.

3. When you connect the dots make sure you know they belong there and how they relate to each other.

Checking Sources

This section is designed as a complement to the discussion in Chapter 2 on vetting sources. That chapter focuses on human sources of information with whom you're communicating, and determining their level of truthfulness. The focus here is written and video/audio sources. In this era of Web-based fact-finding, it principally means that you need to learn to vet the Web.

Charles Seife, a journalism professor and author of *Virtual Unreality: Just Because the Internet Told You, How Do You Know It's True?,* uses an analogy with epidemiology to describe the "disease" of untruth that has infected the World Wide Web.

He says, "What makes a disease scary is how quickly it spreads from person to person, how long it persists, how quickly it mutates and changes."[5] Information that has gone viral can get around the world instantly, persist for years, forever alter our lexicon of search terms, and, true or not, influence our beliefs. He therefore calls digital information an "infectious vector," [6] meaning that is an agent carrying and transmitting an infection—in this case, flawed information—from one person to another.

In a conversation with Jack Devine, former head of the CIA's spying operations and co-founder of The Arkin Group, he gave me an example how this could work with either print or digital information:

> What you have is false confirmation. I give you an opinion about some piece of news in this interview, Maryann. You tell a reporter friend of yours at the *New York Times.* The *New York Times* publishes an article that suggests the opinion is fact. The *Economist* picks it up. I'm sitting here reading the *Economist* and thinking, "Gee, that information I shared with Maryann must really be good because it's surfacing in all these different places."[7]

This phenomenon can occur in simple, silly ways, and incorrect information is then passed around as factual. For example, in 1973, I mis-heard one of the lyrics to "Live and Let Die," the theme song written by Paul and Linda McCartney for the James Bond movie of the same name. Being a smart-aleck student, I told one of my friends about the "fact" that there was an egregious grammatical error in the song. About 30 years later, we happened to be listening to the song and she mentioned that it always bothered her that it contained that error. In those intervening years, I had learned what the actual lyrics were and told her that I had been mistaken in 1973. Of course, when the song came on and she was with another person, she would sometimes point out the supposed grammatical error—with everyone hearing the same thing. My mistake had not only given life to a falsehood, but it had also affected people's hearing!

The disease of untruth even applies to the creation of people. In an NPR/Public Radio International interview entitled "A Web of Doubt,"[8] Seife briefly described the algorithms for producing fake people—that is, friends on Facebook or followers on Twitter who don't exist. One keyword that he said crops up a lot in association with these fake people is "bacon." So the "people generator" might pair the word "bacon" with "specialist" and create a bogus profile. (Seife actually researched how many "people" on Twitter listed themselves as "bacon specialists" and found 2,100. Many of them shared other nouns, including alcohol, pop culture, guru, and fan.) The non-existent person then connects with others via social media and takes on a life of its own; when followed back, the creator can push links or raise the standing of a person or site in search engines. The Motley Fool, a company and Website formed to help people invest more wisely, quantified the problem in an article titled "Twitter's Very Real Fake Problem."[9] The fact that 44 percent of Twitter's 974 million users have never tweeted hints at the problem, but the following numbers give it meaning we can relate to: "StatusPeople's Fake Follower Check tool, which uses an algorithm to determine how many followers are fake or inactive, revealed that 80% of President Obama's 42.5 million followers are fake or inactive accounts, as are 75% of Lady Gaga's 41.3 million followers."[10]

Another common deception is real people creating fake profiles to review books (positively and negatively), argue politics, discredit scientific studies, and much more. Seife calls these make-believe personalities *sock puppets.* In 2012, Facebook revealed that nearly 10 percent of its accounts—83.09 million—were phony.[11]

We don't even know for sure how people really look. Here's a photo of me, used on page 62 of a book I co-authored with Gregory Hartley called *The Body Language Handbook.*

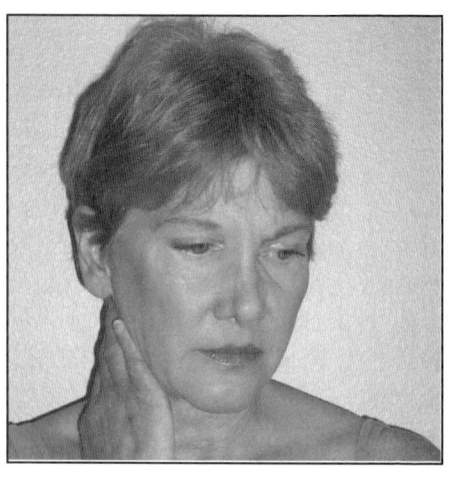

Because the point of the photo was showing my hand doing a self-soothing gesture called an adaptor, I didn't think anyone would call us dishonest if I used Adobe Photoshop to eliminate some of the wrinkles underneath my right eye. If I invest in a better eye cream at some point, then the photo might be an accurate representation of my appearance. This touch-up doesn't have the drama of those done with countless celebrities whose body parts are often slimmer and smoother than Barbie's by the time they show up in magazines. You are not necessarily being mean-spirited if you wonder what a movie star *really* looks like. You're curious; that's a good thing. The paparazzi thrive on the premise that you want to know "the truth."

All of the falsehoods flying from different directions can profoundly affect people's judgment and, ultimately, their beliefs. A good example is the anti-vaccine lobby, well-organized on social media and promoting a point of view, but often presenting it as though it were science. When enough people adopt a point of view, blog posts and articles proffering it as science start showing up. One of the most common messages in the anti-vaccine movement has addressed a link between the measles vaccine and autism. For 12 years, Andrew Wakefield's work gave the supposed link the clout of scientific research. But in February 2010, *The Lancet* retracted the 1998 article by Wakefield, who was found guilty of professional misconduct and stripped of his medical license. Unfortunately, that was 12 years of false information affecting the health and lives of children.

Wikipedia has given contributors the power to *create* facts. To clarify, the information in an entry can begin as a lie, but it becomes true. The mechanism for doing this is to edit a profile with bogus information, use a fake source in the endnote and hope the fact-checkers at Wikipedia don't pick it up (they do try!), wait for it to get picked up elsewhere, and then cite a legitimate source that picked it up in a revised endnote to the Wikipedia reference.

This is how baseball's popular outfielder Mike Trout got his nickname "The Millville Meteor." A fan posted the moniker on the forum pages of a Website—Trout is from Millville, New Jersey—and someone who saw it thought it would be fun to revise the rising star's Wikipedia entry with the nickname. The rest is history. An authoritative source of nicknames and statistics, Baseball-reference.com, picked it up. People began calling Trout "The Millville Meteor." After first expressing surprise over it, he decided to embrace it.

This recounting of how we are so easily duped and deluded by Web-based and other written sources would not be complete without the tale of Ryan Holiday, the man who made reporters at several top news outlets look like the kind of fools who believe a Nigerian prince is about to wire them money. Rather than blame the reporters for being gullible, let's look at how Holiday gave all of us a blast of cold water in the face. If we don't sufficiently question what we're told or what we read, we might as well send our bank account information to the Nigerian prince.

Twenty-five-year-old Holiday subscribed to a free service called Help a Reporter Out (HARO), which sends daily queries from journalists in need of certain types of experts. The categories are just about anything you can think of, from highly technical topics to general interest and pop culture subjects. With the help of an assistant, Holiday pitched himself in response to *all* the queries. In a matter of weeks, he was barraged with requests for his expertise. He became a fount of insights on topics about which he knew either nothing or not much: "Generation Yikes," chronic insomnia, workplace weirdness (pretending someone sneezed on him while working at Burger King), winterizing a boat, and vinyl records. The last piece ran in the *New York Times,* which joined Reuters, ABC News, CBS, and MSNBC among the major outlets falling for his false stories.

No one had done the simplest homework on him, or they would have discovered that his book, *Trust Me, I'm Lying: Confessions of a Media Manipulator,* was set for imminent release. Amazon.com is a great tool for finding out weeks, or even months, in advance when a new book is coming out.

I asked Holiday what advice he would give to people in need of information to avoid being duped. The first of three tips he gave was aimed at journalists: "Don't use services like HARO."[12] With a background in corporate public relations, I can understand his caution. It used to be my job to connect the executives and organizations I supported with current news and journalists writing stories about their areas of expertise. It's tempting to get creative about the relevance of your client's or your boss's expertise to a story. And the closer the reporter got to his or her deadline, the greater were your chances of slipping a quote from your "expert" into the story.

The other two tips would apply to anyone if you broadly interpret the concept of "story":

▶ Don't let sources find you. Find your own sources.

▶ Let the sources influence the story. Don't use the sources to fill in the story you've already written.

Be skeptical about everything you read and hear. This is hard to do for most of us who are (thank goodness) trusting people surrounded by people we can trust. But that reality makes us complacent when it comes to reporting and blogging. I have gone to extremes to document the insights and studies in this book, and provided you with endnotes so you can confirm or challenge my conclusions. But it's possible that I'm wrong about a few things, or that my sources are wrong about a few things. Challenge the assertions. Check your sources.

Using Your Imagination

I learned classic stories related to information analysis in my many visits to the International Spy Museum in Washington, D.C., but none stands out more than historian Roberta Wohlstetter's insights about what happened—and what did not happen—at Pearl Harbor in 1941. In her book, *Pearl Harbor: Warning and Decision,* Wohlstetter lays out the copious facts that indicated that Japan was a threat to the United States and was within striking distance. She asserts that despite having sound intelligence, the United States took no action to avert the attack because of a "failure of imagination."[13] No one in power believed Japan would do what it did. Embedded in that perception was that, to some extent, U.S. leaders focused on the similarities between the United States and Japan in drawing the conclusion that Japan wouldn't bomb a U.S. territory.

Wohlstetter's analysis suggests, therefore, that people may not see the truth, even though all of the elements necessary to see it are right in front of them, because their thinking is constrained. Assumptions, biases, rules, customs, or other factors at play put a box around the analyst's imagination. For example, the suspecting husband concludes that, despite changes in behavior and midnight phone calls, the wife couldn't be cheating because *he* wouldn't do such a thing. The professor assumes that the D student who got an A on the last test just studied hard, instead of giving credence to information that he stole a copy of the test; it's what he *wants* to believe.

Ray Decker has observed successful efforts among CIA, Defense Intelligence Agency (DIA), and other federal analysts to avert failures of imagination. Decker is a retired intelligence officer and federal senior executive who was the director responsible for Combating Terrorism Assessments at the U.S. Government Accountability Office (GAO) before and after the attacks of September 11, 2001. The GAO is responsible for evaluating and assessing federal programs to ensure they are being executed smartly and that there is good stewardship with the funds allocated by Congress to achieve the desired result. Given the agency's mission, GAO analysts have to determine whether or not the programs are achieving what they are designed to achieve. They explore the cause of program failure or inefficiency and recommend solutions for improvement. Part of Decker's responsibility was leading the effort to analyze the capabilities of federal teams responding to terror threats and ascertain opportunities to improve coordination among those teams.

During his decades working with numerous intelligence officers and analysts in the field, he concluded:

> The best analysts I worked with were those who didn't just think outside the box; they refused to see a box. They would look at a problem and not constrain themselves by saying, "This is about aircraft, so I can only think in terms of aviation." No, they would draw from medicine, or sports, or any field that could provide insights about how pieces of information might fit together. They would use any and all approaches to analyze the problem, and not assume that there is only one answer.[14]

When I was in college, I took a course called "Philosophy of Science." During the first week, I followed the lectures and conversations fairly well. For the next 14 weeks, I would sit in class, and much of the time I would wonder what everyone was talking about. My major was speech and drama; I probably had no business being in a class that required some working knowledge of theories in physics and other sciences. The one enduring thing I took away from the class related to the final exam—which I didn't understand. It was a take-home essay with a single question about point mass theory. I was supposed to discuss whether or not it was useful. I think my hands were shaking when I gave the paper posing this question to a friend of mine studying organic chemistry. "What does this mean?" I asked. And then she told me that point masses don't actually exist, though the concept could be really useful in solving certain problems.

Based on that, I wrote an essay and got far more out of the experience than a decent grade. Moving away from point mass *per se,* it occurred to me that introducing an improbable or impossible premise into analysis helps remove constraints. It widens the field of evidence you will see. It arouses curiosity, helping to eliminate the human predisposition to let our unconscious biases shape our assumptions about the cause of a problem or the route to a solution.

For example, on July 17, 2014, the day after a Malaysian passenger jet was shot down over eastern Ukraine, media outlets reported three possible suspects: separatist rebels in Ukraine; the Ukrainian government, which might do that to frame the rebels; and Russia. Analysts working with both technical data and human intelligence would fail in their mission if they simply embraced those possibilities and tried to use imagery, measurements, signals, and information from field assets to determine which one was true.

One of the broad questions analysts would ponder is: "Who has surface-to-air missile systems?" The answer is the United States, Russia, China, Taiwan, Egypt, Germany, Greece, Israel, Japan, Kuwait, the Netherlands, Saudi Arabia, United Arab Emirates, Jordan, Spain, Poland, South Korea, North Korea, Turkey—just about everybody. Given the situation in Ukraine, it may seem ridiculous to even consider most of these countries as the source of the attack, but not considering them is even more ridiculous if you are an analyst. As Decker notes, "A good analyst does not look for the standard answer—in this case, it must be the Russians, it must be the rebels, or it must be the Ukrainian government. A good analyst wants to be able to eliminate other possible answers. In the end, the correct answer may, in fact, be the standard answer, but you have to go through the process of eliminating the others to be sure."[15]

Here's a frivolous example of the value of introducing an improbable or impossible option into an analytic process. Several years ago, while at the Denver International Airport, I decided to get a CLEARcard. It's a photo ID that contains fingerprint and iris data; people who have it speed through security checks at airports that accept it. The person processing me got my fingerprints and then had me stand in front of a machine to do the eye scan. He said, "Hmm. That didn't work." He took me to a different machine and the same thing happened. For whatever reason, he couldn't capture the iris data. He called over his supervisor, who repeated the process, first with one machine and then with another. Same problem. I suggested that my contact lenses were the cause, but they assured me that they took scans of people all the time and contact lenses had never been a problem. I got the card anyway because they had the fingerprints.

The first time I told someone this story, I said they couldn't do an eye scan because I'm from another planet. He laughed and then proceeded to go through all of the reasons he could think of why the scan didn't work. I was fascinated because my story wasn't meant to provoke serious thought; I was just trying to be funny. Since then, I've told dozens of people the story to find out what their reaction would be. With one exception, everyone speculated about the technical and human reasons why the scan didn't work. (The one exception is someone who thinks I might be from another planet.)

And so, by posing an impossible or improbable reason for the failed scan, I've repeatedly aroused curiosity about possible and probable reasons for the failure, as well as a few that are nearly as far-fetched as the extraterrestrial explanation.

You have control over when and how to apply imagination to the analysis of your own challenges, but you may not in

your professional or academic environment. "Failure of imagination" plagues individuals and companies, and sometimes
leads to the demise of entire organizations. Decker points
out that this ties in directly to the nature of the organization's
leadership:

> Many leaders and managers do not appreciate people
> who are contrarians. They don't necessarily appreciate
> answers that upset current policies, viewpoints, opin
> ions, or positions on an issue—which makes it difficult
> for a creative analyst not just to succeed, but also to
> survive.
>
>   An effective leader, on the other hand, will want to
> be surrounded by smart people, people who question
> the status quo, and who do not accept the first answer
> or the easy answer. That makes life a little more dif
> ficult for the leader. There's more thinking involved in
> working with people like that.[16]

In her book, *The Power of Paradox,* Deborah Schroeder-
Saulnier illuminates the practical and massive organizational
benefits of analyzing a problem imaginatively through the use
of one simple word: "and." It's hard for many leaders to rely
on "and" thinking because they rose to their positions of the
authority by making productive either/or decisions. However,
being decisive about choosing X *or* Y, instead of analyzing
whether it's possible to have X *and* Y, often precludes the
leader from looking at the whole picture.

"And" thinking is one type of critical-thinking skill
that helps reduce the possibility of failure of imagination. It
involves the identification of pairs of opposites and determining how they are interdependent relative to a key goal. For
example, a company such as Microsoft or Apple wants to be

known for innovation *at the same time* customers embrace it for its stability. Failure to manage a critical pair of opposite goals like "stability *and* change" results in the company struggling to maintain market share. The worst-case situation—all too common for many organizations—is that one goal is consistently emphasized over the other, and the company begins a downslide from which it may never fully recover.

In her book and supporting Website, Schroeder-Saulnier offers models to help people trying to use paradox thinking to create a complete picture of their situation if they put "and" between two conflicting goals.[17] It begins like this, with two opposing concepts such as stability and change linked by an infinity loop:

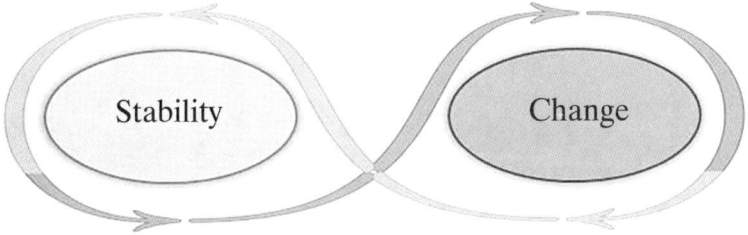

It's then developed step-by-step to arrive at the complete picture, as shown on page 158.

If you were the president of a country, the way your intelligence analysts might use is this by starting with seemingly conflicting goals such as "reduction in force" (coming out of the *domestic* issue of the country's budget) and "escalation of military assistance to an ally" (tied to *international relations* concerns). They would then proceed to flesh out the model to get a picture of how possible that is. Maybe it's not, but the model would organize the information in such a way that "why" should be very clear.

The Aim: What are you trying to achieve?

Action Steps
> These bullets give you actions necessary to achieve the positive outcomes related to change.

Action Steps
> These bullets give you actions necessary to achieve the positive outcomes related to stability.

Metrics
> These bullets are measures that serve as warnings that there is too much emphasis on change.

Metrics
> These bullets are measures that serve as warnings that there is too much emphasis on stability.

Change

Stability

> This area contains bullets listing the positive results of managing change well.

> This area contains bullets listing the positive results of managing stability well.

> This area contains bullets listing the negative results of over-focusing on change at the neglect of stability.

> This area contains bullets listing the negative results of over-focusing on stability at the neglect of change.

The Miss: What's worst case scenerio?

And if you are the vice principal of your local high school, you might start by identifying the conflicting goals of "investing in growth" and "cutting expenses."

Averting a failure of imagination involves systematic ways of exploring "what if?" Your aim, regardless of how you get this outcome, is to remove constraints on your thinking.

Connecting the Dots

Since the attacks on the Twin Towers of the World Trade Center and the Pentagon, the U.S. government has spent billions of dollars to develop mechanical means to improve connecting the dots. Jack Devine, who strongly dislikes the term, is the among the many top intelligence professionals who criticizes this over-reliance on technology to pull together facts to create a picture. He does not see it as getting us closer to the truth:

> By connecting the dots without verifying each piece of information, you can arrive at a conclusion prematurely. When you get to the question of imagination, using an automatic process to connect the dots *reduces* the imagination rather than improves it. You can end up with false information and a lot of extraneous data.
>
> In connecting the dots, you may be linking ideas and facts that have no relationship to each other, cannot be verified, and are out of sequence. If you have intelligence services in Israel, France, and Russia all reporting something, that doesn't make it true. One might intercept the other's communications and add the new information to the mix. That's not verification.[18]

To illustrate Devine's point, consider the following configuration of dots:

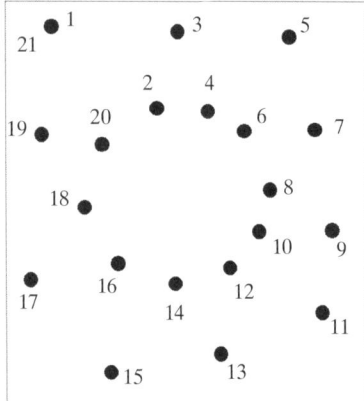 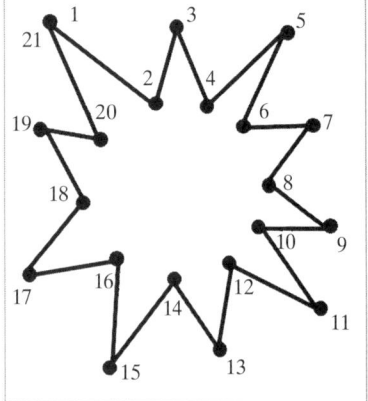

But what if they weren't numbered? Even if each element of the picture were discretely verified, a gap in understanding how they relate to each other might yield a completely different result. For example, let's say that analysis of a situation gives both a firm starting point and a clear sense of last five things that happened. Here is a potential graphic depiction of the result.

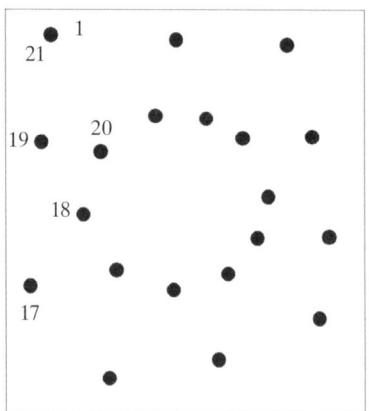 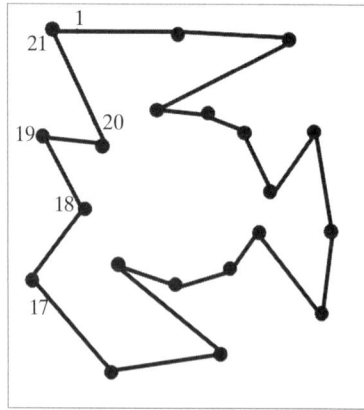

Devine considers this approach a different kind of "failure of imagination"—the kind in which people analyzing available information draw an immediate conclusion from loosely connecting the dots. A variation of this is going into the analysis with a closed mind about the outcome: "If you have a preconceived notion of what the picture looks like, you will drive the data into holes to create the picture you envision."[19]

›››

In summary, analysis is a process that involves verifying data, opening your mind to the full range of possibilities about what that data tells you, and making connections among data only after you complete the other two activities. As a human being, you will not be able eradicate all biases from that process, but, at the very least, you will go into the process with some idea of what those biases are. Your challenge is to manage their influence on the analytical process.

I have coauthored books with 12 different experts and ghostwritten books for another six experts. All of them are people who are recognized in their field, respected as authorities, and extremely bright. They have impressive CVs and resumes, and my bias is to respect their knowledge base and assume they are right—but it's a bias I have learned to fight.

With one exception, they have all given me some tidbit of information that turned out to be inaccurate. They didn't do it deliberately, of course. They simply got one memory confused with another, or had a date wrong, or slightly misinterpreted a concept. This is why I don't automatically accept what they tell me as factual. I second-guess them. I repeat my question to find out if I'll get a different answer. I ask for an example. I do research. And I analyze the information using tools such as those described here.

And even after all that, when the book is in your hands and you're reading it, you might say, "Hey, I was at that event they're talking about and it was overcast that day, not sunny!" As human beings, we aren't perfect with information, but most of us try to come as close as we can to the truth.

In the world of intelligence, that's the goal—not truth in an absolute and perfect sense, but coming close to the truth. In his writings and lectures, Mark Lowenthal, author of multiple books on intelligence and former assistant director of Central Intelligence for Analysis and Production, states that intelligence is not about truth; it's more accurate to think of it as "proximate reality."[20]

PART II

Skills in Action

And ye shall know the truth and the truth shall make
you free.

> —John 8:32, the Bible verse etched into the
> wall of the Central Intelligence Agency's
> original building's main lobby; it's meant to
> characterize the CIA mission in a free society

Even people who want to tell the truth may have problems
with the accuracy of their memory. Memory distortions can
and do occur, and some of them can be considered run-of-the-
mill slips. In other cases, there are either physiological issues
at play or circumstantial evidence giving rise to misinterpre-
tation of what occurred or has been said. Interpersonal skills
and disciplined information analysis will both help you move
toward the truth.

In addition, some people want to tell the truth, but they
aren't sure what it is! This happens in all kinds of personal
and professional situations. A simple example occurred when
I was applying to graduate school. The head of the department
asked me why I wanted to pursue that particular degree. I had
no good answer; I just wanted to do it and had not thought
through the "why." His questions helped me discover my

motivation. Again, your interpersonal, questioning, and analysis skills can help the person move toward a more complete and truthful story.

Sources of Unintended Untruths

When you have cooperative sources sharing false memories with you, they want to tell you nothing but the truth, but for some reason, they just can't. What are the possible reasons for this?

Two University of California, Los Angeles (UCLA) researchers concluded that our understanding of false memories that don't stem from neurological disease is an important window to the non-conscious mind.[1] A key piece of their premise is that after the false memory is generated, people are able to accept it because their non-conscious mind suppresses a brain function that signals uncertainty. So unless you have an unusual amount of control over your non-conscious mind, you probably have as many false memories as the rest of humanity.

Four categories of memory distortion are misattribution, cryptomnesia, source amnesia, and confabulation. The first three involve what experts label false memories—so they can be experienced by any of us—whereas the last one is a neurological phenomenon linked to disease or trauma.

Misattribution

Attribution is the process by which people use information to make inferences about the causes of behavior or events. Misattribution is making an incorrect attribution. For example, you see a waitress pour a bowl of soup on a loud, vulgar male customer's lap. If someone says, "What do you remember?" you state that the waitress was provoked by the man's rudeness and dumped the soup on his lap. The truth is that the waitress had a muscle spasm and accidentally poured the soup on the customer's lap. Your "memory" is actually a misattribution, in that you've linked an event to something with which it really has no connection or association.

Misattribution theory gives us insights into why and how we sometimes deceive ourselves unintentionally as well as why we accidentally convey false information to others. The basis for this is often a strong emotional response to a person or event. For example, a young woman has just made her first skydive. She was attached, facing outward, to the front of her male instructor by a harness. During the skydive, she screamed with awe and delight and, after landing, kept saying, "That's the most fun I've ever had!" Her tandem instructor gave her a big hug and smile and said, "You're the best student ever!" Soon after that, she was in the car with her boyfriend, whom she was going to break up with that evening, but she was still on an emotional high from the skydive. The boyfriend pulled over at a scenic location and invited her to look out at the sunset over the ocean. Then he pulled out a ring and asked her to marry him. She said yes. She had overwhelming good feelings about her day and misattributed her positive feelings at the moment of the proposal to the boyfriend. She was lying to herself, but may not ever realize that that was the case.

A famous example of misattribution involved psychologist Donald M. Thomson in 1975. Thomson went on television one evening to talk about the psychology of eyewitness testimony. The day after the broadcast, police picked him up as a rape suspect after a woman named him as the assailant. It was impossible that Thomson could have committed the crime: He was on television at the time of the rape. The explanation

was a case of misattribution. The woman had been watching
Thomson on television just before she was attacked. She had
mentally replaced the face of the rapist with Thomson's face.

In Thomson's case, it was easy to identify the inadvertent
untruth. It's generally not that straightforward, however, which
is why there are occasional miscarriages of justice linked to
eyewitness testimony.

Misattribution is not a rare phenomenon. It's something
that happens to people on a regular basis, perhaps even daily
for some people. The PsyBlog Website labels the following
three examples of memory distortions "daily misattributions"[2]:

▶   **Misattributing the source of memories.** People
    often say they read something in the newspaper or
    saw it online, when actually a friend told them or
    they saw it in on television or heard it on the radio.
    In a study titled "Retrieval Without Recollection,"
    participants with normal memories regularly made
    the mistake of thinking they had acquired a trivial
    fact from a newspaper, when actually the experi-
    menters had supplied it.[3]

▶   **Misattributing a face to the wrong context.** This
    is what happened in the case of Donald Thomson.
    Studies have shown that memories can become
    blended together, so that faces and circumstances
    are merged.

▶   **Misattributing an imagined event to reality.** A
    1998 experiment by Lyn Goff and Henry Roediger,
    both researchers at Washington University in St.
    Louis, Missouri, demonstrates that memory can
    easily transform fantasy into reality. Participants
    were asked either to imagine performing an action

or to perform it (for example, breaking a toothpick in two). They later repeated the same process. Later still, the researchers asked participants whether they had performed that action or had just imagined it. Those who imagined the actions more frequently the second time were more much likely to think they had actually performed the actions the first time.[4]

What to do

When a person you trust says or writes something to you that doesn't quite fit, you can ask questions in the area of concern—people, places, things, or events. Helpful questions will get the person to put the information into context. These would include questions such as "Sorry—where were you again when that happened?" and "Did you access that photo on your phone? I sometimes find there are color issues with photos on my phone." Focusing on this kind of contextual information can sometimes help shed light from a different angle on the information provided. Or, if the piece of information isn't that important, it helps you move past the misstatement.

Cryptomnesia

It literally means "hidden memory" and it refers to a phenomenon in which you essentially steal from your own memory to create something new in the present. It's unintended self-plagiarism. A classic example is former Beatle George Harrison's song "My Sweet Lord." This song was at the center of a significant plagiarism suit in the 1970s because of its similarity to the song "He's So Fine," made famous by the Chiffons in 1963. Ultimately, a court determined that Harrison subconsciously plagiarised the Chiffons' song.

Cryptomnesia has occupied a central role in controversies over claims of reincarnation and communication with the deceased. William Stainton Moses was a famous 19th-century spiritualist and medium who was caught in an inadvertent lie—and supposedly the first documented case of cryptomnesia—after a séance in 1874 in which he said he had contacted the spirits of two brothers who had died in India. Records provided verification of the deaths, but a newspaper article that had run just days before the séance provided evidence that Moses had drawn every piece of information on the men from what he had read.

Like misattribution, cryptomnesia is a common memory distortion. In fact, University of Georgia cognitive psychologist Richard L. Marsh, who has done multiple studies on cryptomnesia, has concluded that it's "a heck of a lot more common than anybody would realize."[5]

Think back to conversations you've had when one person introduced a memorable word or description. Say someone said, "When the layoffs occurred, my faith in the company cratered." A few sentences later, someone used the word "cratered." This is a form of cryptomnesia, and Marsh offers a reason for it: "Cryptomnesia stems from a failure to simultaneously engage in creative thinking and monitor where incoming ideas are coming from."[6]

In his studies of cryptomnesia, Marsh tried to understand how it affects everyday problem-solving. Not only did he find what he considered high rates of cryptomnesia, but he also figured out when it was most likely to occur. This is an insight that's particularly useful to you in your efforts to get at the truth:

The rate of cryptomnesia was greater under specific conditions. It increased, for example, when there were fewer perceptual and contextual cues—such as the distinctiveness of the voice associated with other-generated information—that participants could use to perform source monitoring during the task, when less time was provided during which participants could monitor the source of incoming information, and when sources of incoming information were more credible. In contrast, plagiarism rates dropped when participants were asked to focus on the origins of their ideas, heightening their awareness of the source of ideas.[7]

Here's how it might work: Imagine yourself in a long brainstorming session with your colleagues at an advertising agency. People have been tossing ideas around for hours, but you are now within minutes of your boss asking for an outline of the campaign for a big client. The boss looks at the outline and says to the six people around the table, "Good work, team!" Susan, the freshman member of the team, beams and gives a big "Thank you!" because she feels that it's really her concept that made the whole thing come together. The boss takes note of her response and mentions it later to one of the other people on the team. "Susan can't take credit for that," says Bob. "If anyone deserves the bulk of the credit it's Ellen. Her Stanford MBA and two years of working with this client really pay off every once in a while." Yet, if anyone were to ask Susan directly about her contribution, she would feel completely honest in saying, "That was my idea."

There is a potentially positive aspect to Susan's plagiarism, though. Marsh theorizes that we can absorb important information this way. For example, he thinks cryptomnesia is at work in many counseling environments. The therapist has been working on trying to get the client to recognize something about his behavior or feelings, but the client has resisted.

Then one day, he bursts through the door with an insight of "his own." His insight is nothing more than personalized expression of what the therapist has been saying all along. Of course, if that is the process by which people sometimes gain important insights, then a memory glitch such as cryptomnesia could also explain the adoption of particular political positions and other points of view.

What to do

The first thing to do is remain skeptical if it seems your source is an unlikely supplier of the information you've received. This is not to suggest that Susan in the previous scenario could not have been responsible for the good idea, or that everyone should assume that the highly credentialed Ellen is responsible. However, if you want the truth, then test the source.

As Marsh suggested, "plagiarism rates dropped when participants were asked to focus on the origins of their ideas, heightening their awareness of the source of ideas." So you might say to Susan, "We all benefit when someone comes up with a great concept like that. We need to be able to replicate the dynamics that give rise to this good stuff. What happened in the meeting that triggered this line of thinking?"

Psychiatrist Ian Stevenson, who was best known for his investigations of paranormal phenomena, remarked at the end of a 1982 lecture he gave on cryptomnesia and parapsychology: "The main lesson we should learn from a study of cases of cryptomnesia is so obvious that it may seem otiose even to state it, but I shall do so anyway: We should be constantly vigilant for the possibility of cryptomnesia in any case when communications about past events are offered for our appraisal."[8]

Stevenson's advice on what to do, therefore, would be to question the veracity of anyone's version of history—autobiographical or otherwise.

Source Amnesia

This is sometimes called source misattribution. So there is a bit of overlap with the discussion of misattribution. It refers to an inability to remember where your knowledge came from. You know for sure that you can ride a bicycle, but you just don't remember exactly how or when you learned to do it, for example.

Many experts would call this a memory malfunction because it indicates a disconnect between two types of memory—that is, verbal memory related to meanings and knowledge (semantic), and contextual, or event, knowledge (episodic). Taken to an extreme, you may recall fictional information as real. For example, your mother may have told you countless times that your estranged father was a violent man, and because of her stories, you actually remember him as a violent man—even though he wasn't.

Some people put the phenomenon to work for them through intense visualization. Because the same brain regions are involved in both visual imagery and visual perception, you are susceptible to perceived visual images as real recollections.[9]

Years ago, Olympic gold medal figure skater Brian Boitano told me the most vivid story of visualization that I've ever heard. It was about his win at the 1988 Olympics in Calgary—after his visualization had given him a palpable sense that he had *already* won. At that moment, his reality fleetingly felt fictional because of that memory phenomenon:

> "The Star-Spangled Banner" was playing and I said to myself, *This tempo is too fast.* My nightly visualizations

for about a year had been complete up until that moment—*exactly* as I'd visualized everything. The jumping, the way the audience responded, the way I responded to the audience. First I did this, then I cried, then I laughed—all that was visualized. When it happened, it was like I was dreaming. It was surreal to me. Then I got up to the podium after winning the gold medal and the National Anthem started playing and I thought, *This isn't the 'The Star-Spangled Banner' that I imagined. It's too fast!* I imagined "The Star-Spangled Banner" going *Daaah, daaah, daaah, daaah, daaah, dah,* but it started differently. The drums came in and it was *dah, dah, dah, dah, dah, dah,* and I thought, *This is not real! The tempo's wrong!* That's what made me realize it *was* real.[10]

What to do

When there is a story involved, try asking questions that break the chronology of it and invite more detail. For example, your source says that his dad was violent and he "remembers" his father coming home from work, going to the refrigerator to get a beer, and then slamming the refrigerator door because there was none. It's actually a story his mother told him many times rather than something he personally experienced, so all he can possibly "remember" is what he's been told. So if you question in your mind whether or not the father was violent you could ask, "What did your dad do right after he slammed the refrigerator door?" You might follow that with a question that takes him back in time in the story: "Did he even put his car keys down before he went to the refrigerator?" After that, you might wonder, "How long did it take for him to calm down?"

Confabulation

Unlike other types of false memories, confabulations have their roots in neurological disease such as Alzheimer's, certain types of strokes, traumatic brain injury, multiple sclerosis, and dementia. People who confabulate are not lying, and have no intention of doing so. They aren't even aware that they are giving you incorrect information.

I had a conversation with my friend's elderly father not long ago. He was an outstanding musician who has been suffering from the effects of *myasthenia gravis* for many years. One of those effects can be cognitive dysfunction. I asked him about a particular, well-publicized outdoor concert that he did 30 years ago, and he related the details of what they performed and the blossoms of the trees at that time of year. The truth was that he had played the concert, but the orchestra did not perform the program he described that night, and it was summer, not spring. Everything he said was true, but it wasn't true about that particular event.

Gregory Hartley, my coauthor of seven books on human behavior, told me a story of confabulation that illustrates one of the reasons why this phenomenon occurs, according to the UCLA researchers: "incorrect mixing of unrelated memory traces."[11]

I once visited an old friend's grandmother in a nursing home. She and others in the ward suffered from advanced cases of Alzheimer's disease. One of the women spoke so brilliantly at times that I kept forgetting her wheels turned differently from mine. She had been a professor at Vanderbilt University in Nashville, and that career defined her. Whenever she drifted into her alternate reality, everything circled back to Vanderbilt. After a while, I forgot she had Alzheimer's disease because she was so charming and articulate. I realized my friend had gone out of the room and asked her, "Did you see where that tall blonde women went?" "Yes," she said. "If you go right out that door there and take a left, you'll be at Vanderbilt. She's at Vanderbilt."

What to do

Unless you're aware of a pre-existing condition with your source, you'll probably have no idea that the memory glitches you detect are confabulations. All you really can do is proceed on the assumption that your source wants to be cooperative and ask questions accordingly.

If you have a cooperative source—someone you are confident wants to tell you the truth—avoid criticizing the person's memory, judging the person's character harshly, or badgering the person. Ask questions that help the individual put information into a context; establish links among persons, places, things, and events in time; and express emotional responses to events and people that help you understand why you may have heard some false memories.

Managing Sources Who Grope for Answers

In many environments, such as medical and legal/law enforcement, people often want to tell the truth, but they are grappling with uncertainty or confusion about how to explain something, and/or they feel intimidated by the professionals asking them questions. Rapport-building skills, good questioning, selecting the best conversation motivators, and reading body language all come into play daily for many people in these environments. From the person who greets people in the reception area to the most senior individual (doctor, lawyer, CEO, detective, and so on), *everyone* in the environment can impact the ability of the source to tell the truth.

Without the truth, the repercussions can be profound: A person's health might be at stake, or an investigation could be stymied, or a dangerous product defect could go undetected. But truth-telling isn't just an action that averts disaster. Depending on the context in which you operate, there are also financial benefits to having your clients, customers, constituents, and coworkers level with you.

Harvey Austin has been a board-certified plastic surgeon since 1970 and he built a thriving cosmetic surgery practice in a Virginia suburb of Washington, D.C. In fact, the Austin-Weston Center continues as the largest non-university cosmetic surgery practice on the east coast of the United States. Over a period of years, I had many opportunities to observe his staff in the office and in the operating room because I was writing a great deal about medicine and surgery at the time, and Austin was generous in granting me access. I also interviewed a number of his colleagues and observed some of their practices, as well. In addition, I had an opportunity to experience Austin's highly effective client screening process because I first came to the practice as someone seeking a cosmetic procedure.

For clients who were a match for the practice, the screening process almost invariably was the start of a positive experience. At that first consultation, we were guided to a state in which we felt non-defensive telling the truth about why we wanted Harvey Austin to change our face or body. It's a potentially emotional experience wherein people might readily hedge on what's motivating them. For example, a woman might say, "I just want to take 10 years off my face," but what she really means is "I want to look as young as the woman who's been seducing my husband for the last six months."

For those who were not a good match for the practice, the relationship was suspended at that initial consultation, regardless of whether or not they thought they wanted to move forward. At that moment, they wanted a cosmetic procedure to fix an emotional problem. With a high degree of certainty, Austin's staff could determine who would thrive during and after the cosmetic procedure, and who would be disappointed and/or litigious no matter what happened.

Austin monitored the results of this vetting process quantitatively and qualitatively:

> We counted all the surgeries and divided it by all of the people we saw. Year after year, it was 43 to 46 percent. Every once in a while, someone would say, "Don't you think we ought to get that percentage up higher?" And I'd say, "Hell no! It's where it ought to be. Those people outside that group are the people who, out of our consultation, we help them to decide that this is not the right place or the right time for them."
>
> We always wanted to operate on the people for whom the operations would make a difference in their life and not operate on those people whose cosmetic surgery, no matter how well handled, would make no difference at all.[12]

In getting to know Austin and his staff, I learned that almost all of them had taken personal development courses. That piqued my curiosity about whether Austin hired people on the basis of their existing interpersonal skills or trained them in aspects of human behavior. He said, "Both." Then he explained key criteria he had for his staff in these terms:

> Cosmetic surgery is highly feminine. The fewer men we had around, the better. We wanted to create a sorority. So I wanted bright, presentable women of no particular age who had been great waitresses. To get a

lot of tips, you have to realize that however great you were with one table, the next table doesn't really care. You have to start from scratch constantly. You have to be able to get along with every person who comes in to order and with the people who work there.

Another aspect of being a great waitress is that it doesn't matter if she makes mistakes; it's a matter of how she cleans them up.

The third aspect is good service—and part of that is opening possibilities by asking helpful questions. A waitress just doing her job would say, "Hey, what do you want for dinner?" A waitress who cares about her customers and loves doing her job says, "Hi, it's really good to see you! Would you like a before-dinner drink? I can bring you some nuts and cheese with that." And before they can even wonder where she is, she shows up and says, "And as for the main course, let me tell you what I'm getting the good feedback on." Later on, at just the right time she asks, "And would you like dessert? Or maybe a cheese platter?" In other words, she knows all about service.

Service is about opening up a possibility for others that gives them the opportunity to step in and take action.[13]

Austin didn't literally just hire waitresses, but the metaphor is useful because the type of person he described is someone who knows how to build rapport by making others feel special and cared for—someone who helps clients feel energized and focused about taking action. His staff knew how to make a potential client, who may be reticent about why she was there for plastic surgery, trust them enough to admit the truth. The woman who ultimately admitted that she wanted to look 10 years younger to compete with her husband's mistress would not make the cut—at least not at that first consultation. Once people in Austin's practice realized that someone had a vengeful, supercilious, or other misguided motivation for wanting cosmetic surgery, that person would be respectfully encouraged to seek help elsewhere. In short, those women needed therapy either instead of, or prior to, cosmetic surgery.

The practice's effective screening—which averted costly malpractice suits—not only relied on the interpersonal skills of the staff, but also on a system of client evaluation that included good questioning and stress detection. My first interaction, which happened many years ago so the dialogue is my best guess (see prior sections on memory distortions), had highlights such as these:

After being greeted and escorted to an office by Carol, we sat down with no barrier, such as desk, between us.

Carol: How did you hear about us?

Me: I was referred by (name of a close friend).

Carol: How is she doing? I remember she was going to audition for a movie being shot in Baltimore.

Me: She's great! She just did a bit in that movie that should grab some attention.

I was impressed with the fact that she remembered my friend because it was such a busy practice. We probably chatted for a while before she asked her next question about having my nose reshaped.

Carol: Why do you want to do this?

Me: I sometimes look in the mirror and see a stranger. For some reason, this face just doesn't seem to be me.

Carol: How do you see yourself inside?

This was a pivotal question and it is one that I remember distinctly from the consultation. Carol got me to open up about a personal vision of myself. It was the truth about who I thought I was.

Having addressed the "why" question, we went on to the other critical interrogatives: what the surgery entailed, when we could schedule it, who would take care of me. Questions also addressed my expectations of what I would look like, as managing those expectations is an important job of staff in this environment. Carol also asked me questions to determine how healthy and health-conscious I was. And probably most importantly, we laughed about quite a few things. As Austin said when I spoke with him, "We wanted to see smiles on our staff and smiles on the people coming through and going out the doors."[14]

The challenges of a questioner in a medical environment like Austin's and in a legal or law enforcement environment are analogous. There is a high likelihood that the individual has some degree of stress; the ability of the questioner to build trust *before* questioning is critical in getting the truth from that person.

In many cases involving violence, medical professionals and law enforcement have to come together and build that trust in a coordinated way prior to questioning and subsequent legal proceedings. The good news for these professionals is that research suggests that memories of traumatic events tend to be accurate because emotional experience heightens memory. There may be short-term memory issues, but once the person has had at least a few days to rest and recover, the rapport-building and questioning of skilled professionals can often arrive at the truth.

Sue Rotolo holds a PhD in nursing and has served as a sexual assault nurse examiner (SANE) for 22 years. These nurses are certified forensic nurses with a specialty in working with patients who have reported sexual assault and collecting evidence related to the assault. They sometimes are called on to testify in court as expert witnesses. Rotolo has a rare breadth of experience because of holding certifications in adult, adolescent, and pediatric practices.

Trust-building begins before a SANE nurse ever meets the patient, and the law enforcement professionals who first attend to the patient engender this. When a patient reports a sexual assault, she learns she is going to be seeing a healthcare provider specially trained to help patients who have been assaulted. That knowledge predisposes the patient toward positive feelings about the interaction. She has some reasonable assurance that she will be in the company of a compassionate and skilled person who is there for her in an exclusive and private way.

In many cases, alcohol or drugs might be involved, so the patient might try to alter some of the facts to make them look a little better. She doesn't want to be judged as someone who invited the rape because of where she was or what she was doing. Some assault victims have already judged themselves; they come to the exam with guilt that they "let it happen" because they were drinking or hanging out with a bad crowd. Another reason to minimize the involvement of drugs or alcohol is that the victim does not want to be perceived as lying about the assault because she was under the influence of some substance at the time.

The nurse makes it clear that being truthful has huge value to her as well as to other women she might help later. "We let them know that nothing is going to surprise us and that they are not alone."[15]

But even after expressing compassion, understanding, and competence, a SANE nurse is dealing with a woman who probably *can't* tell her the whole story; she just isn't mentally capable of it. New research indicates that a patient who has gone through an assault is probably better able to remember details of what happened after she's gone through two sleep cycles.[16] That might not be two days, because it could be several days before she completes two sleep cycles.

The reason may be the person has been in shock, with the body experiencing extreme fight-freeze-or-flight responses. The process of normalizing would involve a series of steps, perhaps beginning with a 911 call, then going through the initial medical and law enforcement procedures—all the while with the victim saying to herself, *If I can just get through this....* After a couple of days, she has gone through it, and the body and mind start to calm down a bit. At that point, she can remember more details.

Knowing this research exists, healthcare providers and law enforcement personnel would not assume that a story that differs from the one they heard immediately after the assault means that the victim was lying, or is now lying.

The rapport-building of a SANE nurse would be geared toward establishing a sense of safety and trust, so "easing fears" would be valuable conversation motivator in conjunction with direct questioning, whereas something like *quid pro quo* would not. "It's not about us. It's about them," says Rotolo,[17] and a *quid pro quo* that implies "I've been there, so I understand" is completely inappropriate. The SANE nurse understands because of her professional experience, and it's that combination of competence and compassion that helps the victim feel connected to her. Rotolo says: "We focus on how powerful it is for them to tell us what happened. There is a lot of empowerment for them in sharing the truth of what happened with us. They come to understand that they help us care for them when they tell us everything and they help us care for others."[18]

At the beginning of the exam, the nurse makes it as routine as possible and does things the patient would normally have done in any checkup—blood pressure, temperature, and so on. These are "little touches" that help the nurse move toward the examination of areas of the body that have been assaulted. While this is going on, the nurse tries to get the patient to begin the narrative of what happened to her and, of course, asks for her consent to touch her. It's important that the patient feels she has control over whether or not someone touches her. As the exam progress, questions arise based on what the nurse sees and hears. So the process of questioning and conversation is continual throughout the exam. According to Rotolo:

> Sometimes there is a victim advocate in the room who are skilled in giving emotional support while the genital part of the exam is occurring. Even photographs of the assaulted area may need to be taken, but by the time they are taken, most women feel enough trust for the nurse that they realize they are necessary and consent to it. They feel protected.
>
> You can't put any judgment on the way they are acting at the time of the examination. Everyone is little different emotionally and cognitively. On one end of the spectrum, some women have had such horrific things happen to them in life, that this is just one more horrific incident. I had a young girl come in after a sexual assault and she was fabulous during the examination. We were talking comfortably and she said matter-of-factly, "You

know, my mom's been raped. My aunt's been raped. It was just a matter of time before I was." She was aware of what happened.

You can't say if someone is laughing during an examination that she's lying. You can't say because she's crying that she's lying. There is no typical reaction.

In the past, we used to put a lot of weight on their reactions. That's gone by the wayside. Thank goodness.[19]

Rotolo's comment prompted a story I had long forgotten: A college friend of mine had been raped. Before the incident, she asked the assailant if she could put in her diaphragm. He agreed, and then proceeded to rape her. Back when that happened, as Rotolo notes, a common perspective was that a woman who thought enough to protect herself by asking for the assailant to use a condom or other form of protection perhaps wasn't *really* raped. Fortunately, as a society, we've moved past that stupidity. The truth is, just because a woman tries to protect herself when she's being assaulted in no way diminishes the violence of the attack.

Relative to the specific challenge of crime investigators, research published in *Applied Cognitive Psychology* shows that "the additional time spent on building rapport (in particular using verbal techniques) may prevent inaccuracies in witness accounts and decrease the witness's susceptibility to post-event misinformation."[20] The lead author, Jonathan P. Vallano, explains:

> When police interviewers build rapport by creating a comfortable environment with a witness, that witness is less likely to report false information than a witness that has not benefited from a comfortable

environment. Our study, based on accounts from over 100 college-aged adults who viewed a videotaped mock theft crime, shows that building rapport before these adults were asked to recall the mock crime decreased the percentage of inaccurate information reported by these witnesses.[21]

Vallano also pointed directly to the value of *quid pro quo* in this trust-building process—but this would assume that the circumstances of the interaction were very different from those described by Rotolo and her interactions with a victim immediately after an assault: "We found that when the investigator shares something about him- or herself with the witness, the person being interviewed is more likely to trust the interviewer and disclose a higher percentage of accurate information in return."[22]

Insights like Vallano's are valuable, but the problem is they may not always make it into the hands of professionals on the front line. According to an article in the *International Journal of Law and Psychiatry,* "Police officers receive little or no training to conduct interviews with cooperative witnesses."[23] They noted that the same could be said for most accident investigators, attorneys, physicians, fire marshals, safety inspectors, and many others. The big difference among them in terms of going after the truth is that they deal with different content.

The Cognitive Interview

Ronald P. Fisher and R. Edward Geiselman are researchers who have written extensively about investigative interviewing and developed something they call the cognitive interview (CI).[24] They introduced it in a book called *Memory-Enhancing Techniques for Investigative Interviewing,* and then focused the application of CI on police work in follow-up work. CI was designed primarily as a tool to help investigators improve their interviews with cooperative witnesses and victims, although many elements can be applied, or adapted to apply, to people in other professions where the source is stressed out. Fisher and Geiselman organized their method around three psychological processes: cognition, social dynamics, and communication.

Much of what they describe in their method integrates techniques and insights discussed earlier in this book. The following are highlights of CI.

Cognition

This facet of the method focuses on memory retrieval and the interviewer's concurrent challenges of connecting with the source, following source leads, and good record-keeping.

» It's important to encourage the person to re-create what happened mentally. That would include every aspect of it (physical, mental, and emotional) because all are part of the truth. Fisher and Geiselman encourage an empathetic response, but they discourage either termination of the interview (if the source gets emotional) or instructing the source to draw back from emotions. Interrupting or stopping the interview may make the source feel patronized or as though he or she is being denied an opportunity to be honest about everything.

» We all have a limited ability to process information, but people who are feeling a great deal of stress have a diminished ability. Your source might have trouble following your questions, interpreting them, or processing his or her answers to them. Don't overload the person by asking a succession of questions without allowing the person to take his or her time and answer each one fully. Be really mindful of avoiding any of the so-called bad questions—compound, vague, negative, or leading. Use the conversation motivator of silence rather than interject another question or a comment while the person is thinking.

» Each person's mental record of an event is unique. Some of this has to do with *access senses,* meaning that some people are highly visual, whereas others are auditory, and others might lead with their kinesthetic sense. Still others might have their primary memory be the smell of flowers or gunpowder. It is vital that you customize questions for the source rather than just ask standardized questions. Listen to the person's narrative to help you decide what his access sense(s) might be.

» Fisher and Geiselman call this aspect of CI "witness-compatible questioning," and there is more guidance on how to do that in the next section on tips to help you structure questions. Fisher and Geiselman assert that witness-compatible questioning is probably the most difficult aspect of CI to learn, and that's because it requires the questioner to pay attention to the source—her character, her nature, and how her emotions and level of cooperation might change during the interview. So much of the success of CI reflects what has been covered in many ways in this book: rapport-building.

» The next piece of CI is something that I tell my coauthors and contributors all the time: You can tell me a story again, even if you know you told it to me before, because something new will come out of it in the retelling. Never say "You already told me that" to a source. If you want the truth, listen to the story again. And again.

» Recall accuracy is important, so if your source starts to wander off—think back to the eye movement clues that may indicate imagination rather than recall—then just say, "It's okay to say that you don't remember."

» The final guidance in the cognitive section relates the source of false memories described earlier as either misattribution or cryptomnesia. In this case, the source may construct a more complete story than the one he actually remembers by incorporating details he's picked up from other sources—including you, if you ask leading questions. Or, he may have seen something on television that crept into his subconscious mind. Refer to the "what to do" suggestions earlier in this chapter if you suspect either of these memory glitches.

Social Dynamics

Questioner and source are part of a dynamic social unit; each influences the other in the way the two interact. To have an ideal outcome, the roles should be coordinated. The recommendations that Fisher and Geiselman make relative to this topic dovetail precisely with has been recommended earlier in this book—namely:

▶ Build rapport.

▶ Engage the person's natural curiosity through both open-ended questions and listening.
    Hopefully, get the source to ask questions, as well.

▶ Use conversation motivators such as "boosting ego" and "easing fears" to keep the source feeling positive about himself.

Communication

The questioner has a need for information, and the source theoretically has the ability to meet that need. The techniques recommended by Fisher and Geiselman, once again, dovetail closely with what intelligence experts advised in Part I of the book:

▶ Ask questions that help the source focus on all aspects of the circumstances—people, places, things, and events. If one of these areas of investigation seems lacking, then head there with your questions. This doesn't mean that the source should feel constrained, though. If she wanders off topic, just return to the topic later and listen for what's revealed in the meantime.

▶ Non-verbal output counts as information, as well. Body language can reveal the emotions that perhaps words cannot. In addition, in dealing with crime or other circumstances in which visual detail is an essential part of the story, moving around or drawing can help the source tell you everything you need to know.

〉〉〉

Fisher and Geiselman didn't merely use the CI method in the laboratory to validate its effectiveness. They tested it with officers handling real crimes. Those field studies showed the same pattern of effectiveness as did the laboratory studies.

Tips for Structuring Questions for a Cooperative Source

In the example of the cosmetic surgery practice, the first victory in eliciting the truth from clients is building rapport so that the people seeking a procedure do not feel defensive about their motives for wanting cosmetic surgery. The hope is that even those who are not a fit for the practice are well-served by the consultation. Similarly, in the law enforcement example, the first task of investigators is to build trust, not to go directly down the path of mundane demographic or case-related questions.

A questioning style that reflects an understanding of what the source is likely to respond to—ego boosting, incentive, and so on—supports that initial rapport-building. Ideally, the questioner would also have a sense of the person's *information sorting style.*

Dean Hohl is a former U.S. Army ranger and leadership consultant with whom I wrote *Rangers Lead the Way.* He developed a succinct way of describing information sorting styles. Following are three styles that can guide a questioner in knowing how to get additional salient information from a source:[25]

» **Large chunk vs. small chunk:** A large-chunk thinker looks at the big picture; he thinks in conceptual wholes. The opposite type is someone who focuses on details and thinks in small pieces.

  ▶ A lawyer questioning a friendly witness might begin by asking him to tell everything he knows about the case. If the witness is a large-chunk thinker, that narrative might be a "high-altitude" view of what happened and who was involved. Diametrically opposed to that would be the narrative of a witness who is nose-in-the dirt with his information. It's a narrative stuffed with details.

  ▶ Someone questioning large-chunk thinker keeps moving forward with good follow-up questions, the most basic of which is "What else?" or "Who else?"

▶ People who are extremely focused on the bits and pieces instead of the whole have a tendency to add peripheral information that has no direct link to anything else in the narrative. A questioner with the small-chunk thinker, therefore, needs to ask questions that clarify links between pieces of information. The categories of information are people, places, things, and events, so follow-up questions would help sort the details into those categories to make it easier to see how they tie together.

» **Sequential vs. random:** The sequential thinker wants her facts well-organized, and she's very process oriented, preferring to finish one thing before starting another. A random thinker feels comfortable jumping from topic to topic.

▶ In terms of storytelling, the sequential person will have some underlying organization that should be apparent. It might be a moment-by-moment chronology, or, if the person is a large-chunk thinker as well, the story might be presented in terms of a sequence of major events. A random person may go in and out of chronology, possibly hitting on highlights first and filling in missing parts of the story later. Asking questions of a random person that channel her into more sequential thinking can help fill in gaps or correct misperceptions. Conversely, asking a sequential thinker to jump around a story can also help you check the soundness of her story by taking a close look at different pieces of it.

▶ The earlier sections in this chapter on false memories include some "what to do" tips that can be enhanced by understanding sorting styles, such as sequential and random, and how you might shift your questioning based on that knowledge.

» **Approach vs. avoidance:** The person characterized by an approach orientation tends to move toward opportunity and situations that satisfy curiosity. In a situation involving some risk, for example, he'd automatically consider what the rewards might be. The avoidant person tends to move away from a perceived danger or the unknown, telling himself, *Don't do this because of what could happen to you.*

▸ Leading with the "childlike curiosity" conversation motivator should be very effective with someone who has an "approach" view.

▸ In questioning an avoidant source, the conversation motivators of easing fears and engendering a sense of certainty should support your rapport-building. HR professionals, physicians, police, counselors, or anyone else facing people who might be asking questions of a cooperative avoidant source need to offer emotional, psychological, and, if necessary, physical protection. You will help foster the person's feelings of security and trust in you.

The sequence of working with a cooperative source is the same as it is with anyone who wants to hide something or is blatantly hostile. Start by cultivating trust—that is, build rapport with the person. Ironically, in trying to get the information you want from someone who is accommodating, there is a tendency to downplay the importance of this. If you have an information need for a negotiation, investigation, personal relationship, or any other circumstance, make sure the trust is there before you ever unleash your questioning skills.

People who think everything is relative when it comes
to truth are doing a great deal of harm to society. If
there's no truth, you can set your own rules. Truth
is the way things are. It is what is real, not what you
want to be real. You've lost theologically, you've lost
morally, you've lost in every single way if you don't
think there is absolute truth.[1]

—David Major,
Retired Senior FBI
Supervisory Special Agent; first director of
Counterintelligence, Intelligence and Security
Programs at the National Security Council at the
White House

A clandestine officer goes through the process of identifying,
vetting, and cultivating sources to do everything possible to
secure a loyal supplier of information. Even so, there may be
lingering questions about the degree of loyalty, whether or not
the source is telling everything he knows, or whether he might
be tampering with information. In the context of covert operations, these sources who volunteer or who are recruited by a

case officer to provide information or other services secretly to the CIA are called *agents* or *assets.*

Early in his career in the field, Peter Earnest discovered that a valuable agent with whom he'd maintained a good relationship showed signs of playing fast and loose with his information. What Earnest did is *not* something you should try at home, but it does demonstrate one way to get the truth without actually asking for it.

The asset was known for producing lengthy, detailed reports. In the course of reviewing his reports, Earnest noticed similarities between the material the asset reported and what the station was getting from the intelligence services of certain other countries. The similarity put Earnest on alert and triggered the question: Is he talking to them as well as us?

He decided to leverage his good rapport with the asset to determine to what extent he and his information could be trusted. For years, the asset had invited Earnest and his wife to dinner. Not wanting to mix business and pleasure, he had always declined. During a routine discussion with the asset after suspicions had surfaced at the station about his reporting, Earnest moved the conversation to friendly territory; that prompted the asset to issue another invitation to dinner. Earnest accepted.

The asset and his wife lived in a kind of townhouse. Although the exterior was drab, the residence itself was well-appointed. He escorted his guests to the living/dining area upstairs. Earnest's aim was to get to the office downstairs, where they occasionally had meetings. At another meeting just before this dinner party, Earnest had had a chance to examine the desk and determine that there was space between where the drawer of his desk closed and the end of the desk. When the asset had left the room briefly, Earnest was able to figure out that the space would be a good spot to plant a microphone.

Unfortunately, this was not a pin-sized bit of 21st-century recording technology. The 20th-century mic that Earnest brought with him to dinner that night was embedded in a foot-long wood block with batteries and a transmitter wired into strapped to his leg.

Fortunately, the asset and his wife had invited another couple so there were introductions and polite get-to-know-you conversation that extended the early part of the evening. Earnest had told his wife that when he excused himself from the party to go to the bathroom, she had to keep the conversation lively and distract the asset.

He knew there was a bathroom downstairs, so that's where he headed. After sneaking into the office, he got under the desk, lay on his back, aimed the silent drill he'd hidden in his suit, drilled holes near the back of the drawer, and installed the bug. He scooped up the sawdust that had sprinkled down on his chest, put it in his pocket and rejoined the party.

For weeks after that, Earnest and his colleagues at the station monitored the asset's conversations. Evidence was conclusive that the asset had been collaborating with multiple other intelligence services.

Without telling the asset why, Earnest ended the relationship with him. But it wasn't just a matter of the man's integrity; it was a matter of whether or not the CIA was not only getting the truth, but was the *only* intelligence service getting the truth—part of the criteria for cooperation with the asset. Earnest explains:

> The business of intelligence is to get information that meets certain requirements and if it means dealing

with the devil to get it, well, so be it. If the agent had been giving us critical information, we might not have dropped him, regardless of his triple dipping. It wasn't and whatever value it did have was diminished by the fact that multiple competing organizations had it, too.

There are circumstances that might even drive us to say, "We know what you're doing and we will pay you more to drop your other customers." We wouldn't tell him how we knew; we'd fabricate a story that wouldn't suggest that we had mistrusted him. With a move like that, you might be buying time, you might be buying loyalty, or you might be buying trouble. In the spy business, as well as whatever you do, you have to consider all the options, but in the course of that, make an exhaustive list of the repercussions of choosing each option.[2]

Before looking at the non-spycraft ways—no hidden mic, no disguises—to get a source that is hiding something to deliver the truth, consider how Peter Earnest's experience ties directly to a common business scenario. Let's say you are one of two copying/printing businesses in a small community. A vendor has been supplying you exclusively with inexpensive ink cartridges and she gives you a deep discount on photo-quality paper. You find out through your sources in town that the vendor has decided to give your sole competitor in the community the same incentives to do business with her. You're upset, because the products you'd gotten from your supplier had given you a competitive advantage. Your options are to continue with the supplier and look for a competitive advantage in another area of your business, try to find a new vendor, or confront the vendor and give her an incentive to stick with your previous exclusive arrangement. Your decision depends on the value of what you're getting from the supplier.

Now think of the scenario in terms of information in your workplace. Is a prickly relationship that yields good insights and gossip worth tossing out because you aren't the only one hearing them? Or, do you want to manage the relationship to get whatever you can from this source that often has something to hide?

Assessing the Partially Cooperative Source

You can set your source up with verbal and non-verbal tests and watch for the cues of deception to determine if your source is hiding something or twisting the truth. Chapter 2 covered the topic of verbal and non-verbal red flags; the insights in *this* chapter are complementary but focus more on the "what else"—that is, what else you look for once you have a suspicion that you are being deceived through omission or distortion of facts.

Verbal Tests and Cues

You can quickly get signals of deception from avoidance of a yes-or-no question, as well as gaps or substitutions in storytelling.

Avoidance of yes-or-no questions

The questioning techniques that Jim Pyle and I covered in *Find Out Anything From Anyone, Anytime* centered on structuring questions that require a narrative response. This is an essential skill in baselining your source, rapport-building, and extracting facts. In probing for the truth, however, it's sometimes useful to ask a yes-or-no question. Lena Sisco relies on a "rule of three": In general, if you ask a particular yes-or-no question three times and don't get a yes or a no, then the person is hiding something. It might just be that the question arouses so much sensitivity in the person that she can't bring herself to say simply yes or no.

Here is a re-creation of an exchange between a 62-year-old, attractive single woman who prides herself on being an old-fashioned Southern belle and a journalist. (By "Southern belle," I mean a woman from the southern United States who is generally associated with economic privilege and refined manners.) The question the journalist wanted her to answer was a straightforward one about dating. Keep in mind that a 62-year-old woman in the year 2014 (when I am writing this book) would have been in her prime dating years during the 1970s and 1980s, when women tended to put a focus on their sexual freedom, financial independence, and the fact that they could open doors themselves. The exchange went something like this:

Journalist: I'm doing research for an article and was wondering—have you ever taken a date out for dinner?

Belle: You know I've had very limited means in recent years, so that would be out of the question.

          [*A response like this is an attempt to sidestep the question. The writer asked a question about whether or not the woman had ever paid for dinner on a date, but the woman gave a partial response which focused on only recent behavior.*]

Journalist: Of course, I understand. But I mean 30 or 40 years ago, when you had no financial constraints to speak of. Have you ever taken a date out to dinner?

Belle: Have I ever taken a date out to dinner?

          [*The woman cocked her head as she repeated the question. Repeating the question is another type of evasive maneuver. It buys time. A person who repeats the question is likely hoping that the questioner will get exasperated and move on to another topic.*]

Journalist: Yes. I was just wondering: Have you?

Belle: Men offered to pay. Why would I insult them by insisting on paying?

> [*The woman's downward look indicated there might be some negative emotions associated with the question. She's now had three chances to answer the question, so by Lena Sisco's rule of three, the Southern belle struck out. But in a final attempt to get an answer, the writer approached the question from a theoretical standpoint to confirm or counter her suspicion that the woman's aversion to paying on a date was cultural.*]

Journalist: If you had tremendous means, is taking a date out to dinner something you would do?

Belle: Well, the way I was raised, I would never consider that appropriate.

Words like "never" are not a substitute for "no." Phrases like "I can't" are not a substitute for "no." Answering a question with a question is pure avoidance. Repeating the question verbatim is a delaying tactic.

Many interviewers, some of them in high-profile jobs such as White House correspondent, end up accepting answers like these to yes-or-no questions. The answers that are given are meant to distance you from both facts and truth.

Here is another example, with a slightly different approach, to illustrate the use of yes-or-no-questions and application of the rule of three in a professional situation. This is an excerpt from *Deposition Checklists and Strategies*, a text for attorneys that provides pattern questions applicable to virtually anyone who might be testifying in a trial. The author, T. Evan Schaeffer, offers advice that is consistent with Sisco's:

Sometimes it is hard getting an answer out of a witness. You home in on a particular issue, start to dig a little deeper, and suddenly the witness is fidgeting and pausing and hedging. All of a sudden, he is not even trying to answer the questions are you asking.

Q: You were present at the meeting on August 14, 2005, weren't you?

A: I was traveling a whole lot that month.

It's an answer to a question that wasn't asked. So you start again.

Q: Let me try again. Were you present at the meeting at August 14, 2005?

A: You know, I don't remember *what* I did that day.

Do you give up the point? Of course not. You say, "Thanks for that, but you're still not answering my question. I'm going to ask again..."

And so on. Does this sort of hedging by a witness ever work? Every once in awhile, it probably does. You have to keep asking the question you want answered until the witness answers it. Ask again and again. Usually by the fifth or sixth time, the witness will start getting the idea there's nowhere to hide.[3]

Another way to back off from a yes-or-no question is to use a *dissembling phrase.* This is phrase designed to conceal the truth, such as Bill Clinton's infamous denial of his relationship with White House intern Monica Lewinsky: "I did not have sexual relations with that woman." If the activities he engaged in with her did not, in his mind, constitute sexual relations, then this represented a true statement from his perspective. The problem for former President Clinton is that he was surrounded by people who saw those activities as "sexual relations"; hence, he was ultimately deemed a liar in this instance.

Former U.S. President Richard M. Nixon's testimony to the grand jury about the accusation that he sold ambassadorships is riddled with dissembling phrases. This testimony, which he gave on June 23–24, 1975, remained sealed for 36 years—until November 10, 2011. The grand jury document lists as one of five areas of inquiry: "Any relationship between campaign contributions and the consideration of ambassadorships for five persons"[4] and then names those individuals.

During the Q&A, one of the questioners, Associate Special Prosecutor Thomas J. McBride, asks this somewhat ill-constructed, yes-or-no question: "Do you recall Mr. deRoulet's appointment in 1969, his nomination and confirmation as ambassador to Jamaica?" The exchange then illustrates how Nixon took the grand jury on mental walk through his garden of dissembling phrases and sentences:

Nixon: Well, I think it would be helpful, Mr. McBride, if I were to tell you how I handle ambassadors and how such a document [the exhibit indicating the offer to deRoulet and his acceptance] would come to me so that you can be absolutely certain as to what I do recall and what I don't and why I do not recall.

McBride: Very well.

Nixon: First, noting this date, it was a rather busy time. That was the time we were in the midst of the, one of the great Tet offensives, as you recall. There had been one in '68 and then despite our peace overtures in early '69—there was one that was just coming to conclusion then and Dr. Kissinger and I were developing strategy for his secret meetings which began in August.[5]

Nixon then goes on for pages about how ambassadors are selected and how he was so busy with really important matters that "I must indicate that I paid so—I must say, and I think properly so—so little attention to minor countries that my recollection with regard to who recommended them, et cetera, is quite vague."[6]

The dodging and weaving continues for many more pages until Nixon says in response to the question on the sale of ambassadorships:

> I respond to that question by saying that I have no recollection of ever authorizing the selling of ambassadorships, the making of an absolute commitment for ambassadorships. As I have indicated earlier, my recollection of the entire ambassadorial decision process, which is already in the record, is that those who made contributions would receive consideration, but as far as the specific commitment, et cetera—quote—end quote—is concerned, or the sale of ambassadorships, I have no recollection of using that term or intending that term.[7]

Unfortunately, many politicians have helped numb people to the reality that this kind of answer is worse than a non-answer: It's deception cloaked in language that sounds believable—unless you have skills of truth and of lie detection.

Exercise: Using a Yes-or-No Question

Ask a yes-or-no question of someone you know that is likely to make your source just a little uncomfortable. For example, you work with someone who is bright, sophisticated, and well-read. You might ask her, "Do you ever watch reality TV?" If you get a response like, "Oh, please! Those shows are so stupid," then you know you are on the way with Sisco's rule of three.

You can also try the exercise in conjunction with a conversation motivator to see how often you can break through the impasse created by the yes-or-no question. In the reality TV scenario, you could offer a *quid pro quo* (one type of incentive motivator). You could say, "I know! Most of them really are stupid, but sometimes as I'm flipping through channels, some reality show catches my attention and I stick with it a few minutes." Or, you could try an ego-boosting motivator: "Don't get me wrong: I didn't think for a minute that you would be devoted to any of those shows, but I was curious if you've ever seen one."

>><<

Gaps and mismatches

Ground your evaluation of what you have, and what you might be missing, in the types of information that you can collect: people, places, things, and events. When you hear or read a story, ask yourself if all of those elements seem to make sense individually and together. Questions to ask yourself include:

▶ Is the number of people in the story consistent from beginning to end?

▶ Are the genders consistent?

▶ Are the relationships between characters clear?

▶ Does the location where the person says he was make sense?

▶ Is the description of the place consistent with what I know about it?

▶ How likely is it that the people in the story would actually do what the person says they did?

▶ Does the description of the item in the story sound believable?

▸   Could the events as described fit into the time
    frame?

▸   Does the flow of the story make sense?

Considering questions like this when you hear or read a
story is not a natural impulse if you're in the presence of a
good storyteller. In the theater, the phenomenon of buying into
a story is called the *willing suspension of disbelief.* The trick to
evoking it in real life is having *enough* of a story seem logical
and believable to avert questions like the above from popping
into the listener's or reader's head.

Another factor comes into play that can affect the believ-
ability of a story: appearance. A number of years ago a friend
of mine met a handsome man at a sales conference. He was
one of the presenters at the conference and looked the part
of a senior executive who had every aspect of his life under
control. She was very attracted him. After his presentation,
she approached him, thinking that complimenting him on his
speech would be a legitimate way to meet him. They ended up
having cocktails that evening with a couple of business associates of hers. The man told fascinating stories about college,
military service, and how he founded his company. My friend
was infatuated—so infatuated that she missed an incongruity
in his story. One of her business associates caught it, though,
and mentioned it to my friend later. She immediately realized
that her attraction to the man had greatly inflated her ability
to willingly suspend disbelief.

This is one of the natural human traits that Ted Bundy
exploited in the women he murdered. Attractive and intelligent,
Bundy had been shy in his youth, but he developed a capacity for inventing tales that helped him evolve into a charming man. On occasion, he added helplessness to his charm

by pretending to have a broken arm. His appearance did not arouse skepticism, because many of us have been enculturated to think of evil as ugly.

Exercise: Applying Critical Thinking to Storytelling

Watch a scripted television show or movie (that is, not a reality TV show) with the specific purpose of finding something wrong with it. You're looking for plot holes, character inconsistencies, dialogue that contradicts something previously shown or discussed, and so on. Think in terms of people, places, things, and events to organize your critical thinking.

If you're watching a science fiction movie or a Bond film, don't include technological incongruities such as cars that fly and handheld devices that cure brain tumors. Stick to the story and how it's presented. For example, you may see two people get into an elevator talking about a topic of great concern. Cut to commercial. When the story resumes, the two people are getting out of the elevator and their sentences pick up exactly where they left off before the commercial. Did their mouths freeze in the elevator?

»«

The exercise is good training in not allowing the willing suspension of disbelief to overtake you—but you need to be able to switch gears and immerse yourself in a story when you want to. Otherwise, you'll probably never enjoy any form of theater again as long as you live.

Non-Verbal Tests and Cues

Three different areas of study in the field of non-verbal human behavior offer insights to help you confirm or deny your suspicions about whether or not your source is telling the truth: vocalics, kinesics, and proxemics.

Vocalics

Listening and watching for changes in vocal expression is one way of determining that the fabric of truth has some holes in it. Vocalics is an area of non-verbal communication studies because it's about how something is said rather than what is being said. I'll focus on three facets of vocalics that often indicate emotion and always tell you something about how to interpret what's being said to you: vocal qualities, emphasis, and use of fillers.

Vocal Qualities

Pitch, tone, pace, volume, hoarseness, stridency, and nasality are among the characteristics of a voice. In some cases, they can change from moment to moment, reflecting a deviation from the speaker's baseline.

» **Pitch** helps convey the intensity of the communication, express a question, or convey uncertainty or even deception. A woman's who's just been crowned Miss Universe will likely say, "Thank you! Thank you!" in a high-pitched voice. And typically, a person's voice will rise at the end of a question (although there are cultures where the opposite is true), so "How long does it take to get from here to Paris?" would have the pitch rise on the word "Paris."

Regarding the expression of uncertainty or untruth, there is often a rise in pitch suggesting that the next thing you should do is agree with him. For example, at the end of a sales presentation, the sales rep might say, "The product is much more reliable than any others" with the pitch rising on the word "others." If this is accompanied by what Gregory Hartley, my co-author on *How to Spot a Liar,* calls a "request for approval" facial expression, then the change in pitch is an important nonverbal signal. It's working in tandem with a facial movement that involves slightly raised eyebrows to suggest, "You believe me, don't you?"

This combination of shift in pitch and a very revealing facial expression is one example of how different types of non-verbal signals often work together to confirm your suspicions about a person.

» **Tone** is a characteristic of voice that goes a long way toward conveying meaning. Most of what I learned about tone, I learned from my mother before the first grade. She would ask me to do something I had no interest in doing and I would say, "Yes, Mommy" in a way that provoked: "Don't you use that tone of voice with me, young lady!"

Tone and pitch work in tandem to convey sarcasm, to clue you in that someone is telling a joke, to leak repressed anger, and much more. They lend nuance to speech to help clarify both the message and the intent of the message. It is their critical role in making sure that a message is understood properly that makes e-mail a dangerous mechanism for trying to be funny or sarcastic. Emoticons can help, but they don't necessarily eliminate confusion.

» **Pace** is the speaking rate someone has adopted in a particular conversation. A sudden change is a deviation from baseline in the context of that conversation and it indicates stress. On a business call earlier this year, I detected that the person I was speaking with had quickened the pace of his speech. I looked at the time and realized that it was about three minutes before 11 o'clock. Even though we had not established an end time for the call and still had a lot of ground to cover in the discussion, I asked, "Do you have another appointment at 11?" He told me did and expressed surprise at the question.

A source who is not being completely honest might either speed up or slow down. Speeding up is one way someone who is trying to deceive you can prevent you from interrupting him with a question or challenge. And if your source suddenly changes the pace by enunciating every word, in contrast to fluid speech that preceded the shift— "I...did...not...have…sexual...relations...with that woman"— you have reason to question the veracity of the statement. Here's another occasion when you are likely to see one non-verbal paired with another as part of the deviation. In the instance of Bill Clinton's denial, he punctuated it by moving his forearm up and down three times in a hammering gesture. This kind of aggressive move was not characteristic of Clinton's normal style of gesturing.

» **Volume** is another vocal quality that conveys intensity. An ardent denial of an accusation would probably be said more loudly than other parts of the conversation. Of course, some people might drop to a whisper in expressing a denial. Neither change would automatically suggest that the person is being deceitful, however. The following discussion below on kinesics gives clues on what kinds of gestures and facial expressions done in conjunction with such a deviation in vocal quality would reinforce a suspicion of deception.

» Qualities such as **hoarseness**, **stridency**, or **nasality** suggest stress only when they aren't normal for the person. When the vocal chords tighten up and/or the throat becomes dry, the voice takes on a different sound. It can get very raspy, the way comedian Joan Rivers sounded all the time; that was part of her baseline. Look for other signs of stress, such as blinking. If the throat is drying out due to a mild fight-or-flight response, then the eyes are drying out, too. You might also see the person's body get more rigid if the vocal chords are tightening. I used to see this combination of tight body/tight voice when I auditioned for musicals in college. If you're really nervous about the audition, you may not hit the high notes (and your dancing won't be that marvelous, either)!

Exercise: Testing Rapport and Emotional Attachment to the Subject

Now that you know some of the vocalic cues of stress, deliberately try to evoke these deviations from baseline. The results might give you a stronger sense of rapport and insight into the source's emotional attachment to the subject:

» During a conversation, make your pitch a little higher and talk a little faster to correspond with your level of animation. Notice whether or not the other person responds in kind. When people feel they have rapport with someone, they have a natural tendency to mirror the other person. If your source mirrors you in pitch and rate of speech, then you probably have a good connection, or at least are on the way to developing one. In contrast, if you sense disinterest or discomfort, that could be an indication that the two of you are not in tune with each other.

» Bring up a topic that involves emotion—positive or negative. If your source is someone at work, then the easiest
way to provoke an emotional response and find out how
it affects vocal quality might be to bring up a common
enemy. That could be a person, an office policy, or a meeting that neither one of you wants to attend. If it's a really
strong negative for the person, you should hear significant
changes in her voice.

» Pay attention to emphasis. Three different messages are
being transmitted in the following sentence depending on
where the person places emphasis:

"*I* did not do that." The speaker is suggesting
that she, as opposed to someone else, didn't do
the act in question.

"I did *NOT* do that." The speaker wants to make
it clear that she denies doing the act in question.

"I did not do *THAT*." The speaker denies doing
the act in question, but she may have done something else a lot like it.

In the course of a conversation with your source, notice
which words are emphasized, but also listen for a lack of
emphasis if you suspect deception. In May, 2010, after former Tour de France winner Floyd Landis admitted he used
performance enhancing drugs and pointed an accusing finger
at Lance Armstrong for doing the same, Armstrong held an
impromptu press conference during a bike race in California.
He said to reporters, "We have nothing to hide. We have nothing to run from."[8]

Oddly missing from his denial was emphasis on keywords.
Also, his delivery was nearly flat.

» Listen for fillers. Typical fillers in English are "um," "uh," "well," "like," and "you know," although fillers are not a distinctly English phenomenon. You will find them creeping into conversation in many languages; American Sign Language contains a gesture for "um," so fillers are not even solely associated with spoken language. In general, such syllables or words fill the gap as you think about what to say next. If you've asked a source a question and get an "um" in response, or if the sentence is peppered with fillers, it could be a sign that person either doesn't want to answer the question or hasn't figured out how to answer it. Watch for movement cues to give you an indication of whether or not stress is present to give you a hint about possible attempt at deception.

»«

Ellen Horne is the Executive Producer of WNYC's Peabody Award–winning show *Radiolab*. On an episode titled "Deception," she contributed the story of a career con artist named Hope, whom Horne termed "very charming." During Hope's trial for fraud, Horne even found herself "rooting for her."

Hope agreed to let Ellen interview her two days before she was to begin her two-year prison sentence, but she rescheduled, rescheduled again, and ultimately cancelled. In one call to reschedule, this is what she said: "Hey, Ellen, it's Hope. It's about *um* almost 3 o'clock and I *actually um* have to change our 5 o'clock meeting. I have to do *something* with my daughter *um* and I'm not going to have time *um* to make it there by five."[9] I've italicized the fillers and words that suggest that Hope had not yet thought through her lie.

Kinesics

Most people would think of this as body language, but because I think of all non-verbal communication as body language, I want to differentiate between the study of movement—kinesics—and other non-verbals.

Eye Contact

Chapter 2 contained a detailed description of ways to evaluate eye movements, which is using eye contact to determine whether a person is engaged, emotional, deep in thought, or conjuring up an idea. In this section, the focus is on using eye contact in other practical ways with your source.

Making eye contact with a person can provoke a response. In a meeting, if you wanted to find out what a specific colleague thought about a idea you proposed, you could present the idea, ask "What do you think?" and then look straight at the person you want to answer the question. This is a common teacher trick: Without actually calling on a person to answer a question, the act of making eye contact indicates without a doubt that you want an answer from that individual. This is a tactic that works very well with silence as a conversation motivator. Make eye contact, pose the question, and wait for a response.

You can send information through eye contact or by refraining from eye contact. After your source provides an answer, for example, your eyes can convey "I'm thinking about that." Combined with silence, or an inert response such as "hmmm," your eye contact may be enough to elicit more information from the person. As a corollary, your lack of eye of contact may convey the same thing since it's common for people to look away—eyes up and off to the side—when they are processing what's been said.

One key piece of information you can send with your eyes is a sense of interest and connection. It's acknowledgment of rapport or the intent to establish rapport. Sustained eye contact while a person is speaking, in conjunction with movements such as nodding the head and slightly leaning forward, are all part of the skill of active listening.

Eye contact has a powerful ability to intimidate, and sometimes that's what you intend. In the Chapter 4 discussion on the use of silence as a conversation motivator, I referred to the one- or two-second differences that different cultures have in terms of how long it takes for them to get uncomfortable with silence in a conversation. These cultural differences exist with eye contact, as well. Whereas people in the United States and Western Europe tend to be very similar, sustained eye contact—and gender is significant here—can be considered inappropriate or even threatening in the Middle East, Asia, Latin America, and Africa. Know what the cultural norms are for your source before trying to use eye contact as a part of your scheme for extracting the truth.

Facial Expressions

"Facial expressions are dynamic signals that transmit information over time,"[10] according to Rachael E. Jack, the lead researcher of a study published in 2014 by a team from the University of Glasgow Institute of Neuroscience and Psychology. They provide a sophisticated signaling system, with Jack's research providing valuable, fresh insights into understanding how facial expression might help us spot stress and other emotional responses in a source.

For decades, the biggest name in research in this field has been Paul Ekman, a pioneer in the study of emotions and their relation to facial expressions. Ekman's groundbreaking work in the universality of human expression identified six expressions of emotion that virtually all people have in common: disgust, sadness, anger, fear, surprise, and happiness. Gregory Hartley, former Army interrogation instructor and author of multiple books on body language and human behavior, identified an additional four: contempt, pride, uncertainty, and embarrassment. On March 31, 2012, Ohio State University announced that a team led by Aleix Martinez, a cognitive scientist and associate professor of electrical and computer engineering, had developed a computational model to identify 21 distinctly different facial expressions that people share: angry, awed, surprised, disgusted, fearful, fearfully angry, disgustedly surprised, fearfully disgusted, fearfully surprised, happily disgusted, angrily surprised, sadly surprised, sadly angry, sadly fearful, sadly disgusted, sad, happy, hateful, happily surprised, angrily disgusted, and appalled.[11]

In contrast, Jack's research reduced the basic number to four. Using Ekman's six as the starting point, her team had study participants categorize random expressions they viewed on a screen as happiness, surprise, fear, disgust, anger, or sadness. Agreement among the participants indicated the expression signaled emotional information. The next step was to establish which muscle movements were associated with which emotions; when those movements occurred figured into the analysis. Happiness and sadness were readily identified. But it wasn't that clear with the other four, which took time to be distinguished, according to the researchers. Ultimately, they paired fear with surprise and disgust with anger: "Early facial expression signaling supports the discrimination of four categories, namely happy, sad, fear/surprise (i.e., fast-approaching danger) and disgust/anger (i.e., stationary danger), which are only later more finely discriminated as six emotion categories."[12]

The value of Jack's categories to you in your efforts to evaluate the truthfulness of your source is that the breakdown can be restated as happy, sad, approach, and avoidance:

▶ If your source is happy, she's either very cooperative or totally convinced she has fooled you.

▶ Sadness would indicate heavy emotional involvement in the topic. You've struck a nerve with your question.

▶ If your question to a source results in the raised eyebrows, open eyes, and slightly open mouth associated with both fear and surprise—even for a flash—you know your approach has pushed her off balance.

▶ If your question to a source results in a lowered brow and a look that says, "Get away from me!" then you know your question has aroused either disgust or anger. She will stand her ground and will likely come across as antagonistic in her response.

Regarding this last point, Ekman has an additional insight on what might be termed "hot anger." His extensive work, also covered briefly in Chapter 2, supports the assertion that there is an anger-reliable muscle at the margin of the mouth that most people cannot control. When it's engaged, the face would conveys genuine anger very distinctly.

Postures and Gestures

In Chapter 2, the four basic types of movements receive attention: illustrators, regulators, barriers, and adaptors. Deviations from what is normal for a person in any of those constitute an indication that stress is present—and stress can be good or bad. An example of good stress is the strong desire to please; an example of bad stress is the presence of fear. As a complement to that discussion, this section focuses on angles and curves.

When I was in British Columbia receiving wilderness training before a 10-day adventure race, I watched a film on what to do if you come face to face with certain kinds of bears. The advice was "Get big!" You square off, put your arms out, and generally try to look as large and angular as possible. The opposite would be rounding your back, shoulders, and arms, and looking as small and helpless as possible. In other words, this is the difference between the posture of a predator and the posture of prey.

If your source adopts a posture of angles—regardless of whether he's standing, sitting, squatting, or lying down—you can consider that assertive. A typical example of an angled posture in a standing position is hands on hips. In a seated position, legs crossed in a figure-four is an angular posture. This is one of the two main postures that Edward Snowden adopted in his May 2014 interview with NBC's Brian Williams. If you already suspect your source is not coming clean, and he adopts postures and gestures characterized by angles, then you have another reason to wonder. You may not have the good rapport that you thought you had with the individual; his body is pushing you away.

In contrast, if your source hunches over, draws her arms closer to her body as though she's hugging herself, or otherwise adopts postures and movements characterized by curves rather than angles, then you have "prey," not "predator." Depending on whether or not you're getting satisfactory answers, you may want to try using an ego-boosting conversation motivator.

Proxemics

This non-verbal is all about how close to or far away from you are to someone and how that influences communication. In general, public space, the kind you probably try to maintain on your walk through a city park, is at least 12 feet. Social space, the kind you establish during a business meeting, is at least 4 feet. Personal space is maybe a foot or so from the body and extends to the social zone beginning at 4 feet. Breaches of personal space, especially sudden ones, can trigger extremely negative responses.

If you've built strong rapport with your source, then that 4-foot mark should be no problem. But what if you lean forward 2 feet and ask a question? Your move can be perceived as an invasive action. Does your source's facial expression convey approach (fear/surprise) or avoidance (disgust/anger)? Does your source suddenly use either a body part—folding arms or turning away slightly—or an object—reaching for his cell phone as a barrier?

The concept of territoriality is also included in this field of study. So even though you may be across the room from your source, when you sit in his favorite chair, you may get the same kind of response as if you had leaned forward and invaded his personal space.

To summarize, if you want to test strength of your rapport, using your knowledge of proxemics is one way to do it.

Evaluate whether your source's response to closing the distance between you and/or occupying territory that is supposed to be under his control sends the signals you had expected.

>>>

To sum up the challenge related to non-verbals, Lena Sisco notes:

> Your job is to pair up what the body is doing with what the mouth is saying. If there is a mismatch, then you have reason to conclude that the person is experiencing stress. Stress can be associated with lots of reasons, but stress can also indicate that a person isn't being completely honest with you.
>
> Behavioral congruency—meaning that the mouth and body match up—suggests truthfulness. Seeing the opposite in response to a question suggests the person is ill at ease with the question and/or her response to it.[13]

Why the Lie?

We would be naïve to think that most people always tell the truth and nothing but the truth. The reality is that most of us are careful about hiding certain types of information and deliberately distorting others. So, though we may often deal with cooperative sources, and we may at some point have to extract information from hostile sources, the most common scenario will be that we want the truth from someone who has something he wants to hide or modify.

It isn't just people who have something to hide who are omitting facts or spinning tales, though. We can understand the motivation to lie of someone who is guilty or embarrassed. But why do even highly accomplished people slip lies into their stories when the truth of their lives is interesting enough?

Dave Major answers the question, "Why do people lie to you when they don't need to?" with a single word: power.[14] There is tremendous power in telling a purposeless lie and getting someone to believe you. It is the kind of power that Ryan Holiday had when he got reports from major news outlets to believe that he was an expert in things he knew little or nothing about. (Holiday is the author of *Trust Me, I'm Lying: Confessions of a Media Manipulator,* who duped the *New York Times,* Reuters, ABC News, CBS, and MSNBC into reporting his "expertise" on subjects about which he knew virtually nothing.)

You are seeing all the signs of being lied to by someone who is not hostile to you and has no apparent reason to lie to you, you could be dealing with someone who simply wants to know he can get away with it.

People who do this habitually are made differently—literally. Yalin Yang, a psychologist at the University of Southern California, used fMRI with test subjects that included documented pathological liars and non-liars. The liars showed an astonishing increase in white matter—23 to 36 percent more white matter than the non-liars—in the part of the brain associated with personality, attunement to other people, planning complex cognitive behavior, and decision-making. It's the part of your brain that supports your storytelling. And the more white matter you have, the better able you are to put bits of information together to fabricate a story. Yang hypothesized: "In the case of lying, it is conceivable that excessive lying repeatedly activates the prefrontal circuit underlying lying, resulting in permanent changes in brain morphology."[15] So all those kids out there who think lying is fun and keep trying to see what they can get away with might be engaged in brain-altering behavior. At least that's one theory. The other is that they were born that way.

Obfuscation in Action

With the tips in mind about avoidance of yes-or-no questions, fillers, and other ways people who want to hide something will fend off direct questions, consider the following exchange from Season 1, Episode 5 of the TV show *24*. It is early in the morning the day Senator David Palmer (Dennis Haysbert) intends to announce his candidacy for president of the United States, and he decides to confront his son about his possible involvement in a murder:

David Palmer: The night of your sister's rape, did you have any contact with Floyd Richter?

Keith Palmer: What?

David Palmer: You heard me.

Keith Palmer: I, I don't believe this. I mean, what brought this up all of a sudden? I mean, let's just leave it all in the past where it belongs.

David Palmer: I'd like to. Believe me. But as it happens, I can't. (*pause*) What did you do that night after you found out that Nicole had been attacked? The truth now. All of it.

Keith Palmer: I don't think you have a right to ask me that.

David Palmer: You don't think I have the right?

Keith Palmer: No, I don't. See, this thing happened. Somebody had to deal with it. But you were in Chicago giving a speech or New York receiving some big award.

David Palmer: Let's deal with my shortcomings as a father some other time. Right now, I want to know what you did after you found out that your sister had been raped.

Keith Palmer: And I told you, I'm not going to answer.

David Palmer: You will answer me!

The nature—not the substance—of this Q&A is something that many people deal with regularly with loved ones, people at work, customer service representatives, and others in our daily lives. And just as David Palmer got to the point of anger with his son because of his son's hedging, so do the rest of us when we don't get straight answers to straight questions.

The insights in the next chapter will help you confirm that you have an uncooperative source. After that, if you want to make progress, you need to adjust your conversation motivators, body language, and rapport-building techniques to accommodate the source and situation.

I don't ask him for anything. I ask him, "Is there anything I can do for you?"[1]

—Eric Maddox,
the Army interrogator who located Saddam Hussein
on his approach to launching an interrogation

MDB.com's one-line synopsis of *The Silence of the Lambs*, the 1992 winner of the Best Picture Oscar, is: "A young F.B.I. cadet must confide in an incarcerated and manipulative killer to receive his help on catching another serial killer who skins his victims." In this case, therefore, it is the hostile source—Hannibal Lecter—who lures the interrogator into a *quid pro quo* exchange that provides her with the truth she needs to catch a killer. Lecter won't simply answer Agent Clarice Starling's questions; he is an intelligent and inventive psychopath who wants to see her stripped down emotionally before he tells her what she needs to know.

Hopefully, you won't have to try to extract the truth from a deranged cannibal, but you will very likely have exchanges with uncooperative sources who want to make you uncomfortable before they give you any information. An all-too-common example is the cheating spouse who wants the wife to feel badly about what she did to hurt the marriage before he comes clean on his infidelity (or vice versa).

In cases like this, you may get the truth, but you aren't the one in control of the conversation. In this chapter, experts tell you how to establish, retain, and regain control so that you secure the information you need. It's all part of the process they describe by which you bring a hostile source over to your side, cut through lies, and extract the truth.

6 Steps to Finding a Dictator

Eric Maddox developed a system for converting hostile sources into cooperative ones that helped him locate Saddam Hussein. Although Maddox went through the the U.S. Army's interrogation training program at Ft. Huachuca, Arizona, he thought the Army method of interrogation was flawed. He incorporated what he determined were effective techniques that he learned at Huachuca into his own interrogation scheme. The process he developed will likely resonate far more with non-military people who face a hostile source because it does not integrate any elements of fear or threat. It relies on:

1. Understanding your source's situation.
2. Identifying his needs.
3. Cultivating trust.
4. Mentally re-orienting the source.
5. Putting the stakes into context.
6. Questioning well.

Understanding Your Source's Situation

Maddox begins by looking at his prisoner's situation; he thinks through the experiences that he had before being led into a room for interrogation. This is analogous to a CEO coming into a meeting with senior executive suspected of financial transgressions and making space in her thinking for the man's circumstances: *He ran an operation in a foreign country, surrounded by people of a different culture, and when I summoned him here for this meeting, he flew 11 hours, put on a suit, and then walked through my door. He is tired and frightened, and probably sees me as calculating and vengeful right now.*

In the venue of the battlefield, Maddox would consider factors such as these: *This prisoner was captured in the middle of the night at his house. When our soldiers went into his home, they didn't know who he was initially. They stayed at his house for about 45 minutes. They eventually put him up against a wall and put a flashlight to his face to suggest that they had an informant with them to help identify him. When they put the flashlight to his face, members of the team kept muttering, "Yes, yes! That's him!" Then they whisked him away to a helicopter. He knows no other prisoners were put into the helicopter. Someone put a hood over his head and he was flown two-and-a-half hours to a location where he's been in isolation ever since.*

In either the circumstance of the prisoner of war or that of the senior executive, the person who wants information from the source has to consider: What was the person thinking? Among other things, he is wondering who gave him up, or how he was found out. In all likelihood, he's also making an assumption that if he is going to be interrogated, under zero circumstances will the person asking the questions help him out. As Maddox says:

It would be ridiculous to think that after you've blown down someone's door in the middle of a war zone, grabbed him by the collar, put a hood over his head, flew him to a prison, and thrown him in isolation for a few hours that he would believe me when I lift up the hood and say, "I'm here to help."

So the first question has to be, "What's going on in the mind of this prisoner?" What does he think he's going to see when I lift that hood? What does he think I'm going to ask him? What direction does he think I'm going to go in?

I want to figure out every possible question and concern in the mind of the prisoner.

One of the initial techniques a military interrogator might use with a prisoner is part of the so-called incentive approach. It might include giving him some creature comforts as a way of getting him to feel more favorable about his circumstances and about the interrogator. Maddox is very skeptical about the value of this—he prefers a strategy that arouses curiosity—because it does not address the core issues related to how the prisoner feels:

Do you think someone who has just gone through what the prisoner went through is going to care about hot chai and bagels? That guy is trying to determine if he should plead complete innocence and try to get the Americans to believe they accidentally captured the wrong person. He's wondering, "Should I marginalize my nefarious activities, by trying to convince him he perceives my activities to be worse than they were? Should I try to negotiate my way out through cooperation? Or maybe I should just sit here and look confused."

Compare Maddox's description of his prisoner's thoughts to how we might describe what's going on in the head of the senior executive under scrutiny. Would a cappuccino and a scone do anything to alleviate his anxiety? Certainly, the circumstances are different in the sense that the executive is not facing an outcome that may be literally life or death, but for someone like him, the possibility of prison time might seem like death.

The key thing to keep in mind that is that beginning of interaction determines, to a great extent, whether or not you will get the desired outcome. Maddox compares it to flying an airplane: if you don't know how to take off, you're just going to crash immediately. "A lot of people do interrogations thinking they are flying the plane and the plane crashed a long time ago." Whether it's an interview, a negotiation, or an investigation like the one with the CEO and her senior executive, the model is the same. You have to begin well, keenly assessing the conditions at hand. After that, you put the necessary speed and direction into the effort so the plane flies.

Identifying Needs

A standard military interrogation begins with an assessment of intelligence gaps and a set of intelligence goals. The interrogator wants to know what information the prisoner can deliver that will help find a valued target, assess military strength, determine battle plans, and so on. So the starting point for the interrogator tends to be what he can get out of the source. That means he is the one going in with needs. That gives the control in the conversation or negotiation to the source, who has the ability to fulfill or not fulfill the interrogator's needs. Maddox takes an inverted approach:

I turn that around, so that it appears I need nothing from him, but he needs something from me. I usually do it in a friendly manner.

I try to seem approachable. I say something like, "Well, there's the guy. Okay, how are you?" He's just come off the battlefield or some other traumatic circumstances. He might shake his head, so I say, "Not good, huh? Are these guys not treating you well? Are you getting everything you need?"

I don't ask him for anything. I ask him, "Is there anything I can do for you?"

He might just offhandedly say that he doesn't belong there. That he's innocent. I might joke, "I know buddy. Everybody's innocent here."

He knows I'm not the one who yanked him out of his house in the middle of the night, so he might think maybe I haven't made a decision about him yet. I'm like clay. I haven't hardened up yet. I'm still shapeable.

The exchange to plant the seed that you don't need anything from the source, but that source needs so much from you, is the basis for going forward. You are laying the foundation for the person to have a reason to speak with you. You ostensibly want nothing, but at the same time can give a lot.

Part of Maddox's strategy in ascertaining needs is that he doesn't have unlimited time. He is in this room and in this meeting to make sure that the source's needs are understood and, to whatever extent possible, met. But he has to leave because of other pressing responsibilities. In the scenario of the CEO and the senior executive who has allegedly done something heinous in a corporate context, the CEO would say that she had to excuse herself due to prior obligations.

The pressure is on. The source must state his needs now or forego the opportunity. And as the desperate intent to forge a connection takes shape, the source then gives verbal and non-verbal cues: *I need your help.*

When people need your help, if you are too strong, you are intimidating and therefore hard to connect with. But if you come across as genuinely curious and serious about trying to understand them and their dilemma, then you are inviting them to connect with you. The ultimate challenge going forward is to ascertain what your source wants. Once that's accomplished, then you have a strong chance of getting the truth from him.

Cultivating Trust

If you're dealing with a hostile source, then chances are good that there is the issue of guilt or innocence at play. As part of his strategy to secure trust, Maddox next goes through a process of convincing the source that he hasn't made any judgment about guilt or innocence. The clear message is that he is malleable and that the information he seeks would be one thing that would help him make some important choices.

The exchange might go like this:

Maddox: I'm really busy. I know they're trying to get you to Guantánamo Bay as soon as possible. I just need to get some paperwork done and make sure I have your name correct.

Prisoner: No, I really need your help.

Maddox: What's the problem? I don't have all day, but I'll do what I can to help you.

Prisoner: I'm innocent.

Maddox: That's not what the commander says. Those guys
           who grabbed you are convinced you're guilty. They
           are happy to have you here.

Prisoner: They're liars. I didn't do anything wrong.

Maddox: I don't know anything about this. You're going to
           have to explain what's going on.

The CEO's exchange with her senior executive suspected
of wrongdoing could easily parallel the above:

CEO: I have to prepare for the board meeting tomorrow
           so you'll have to excuse me. Our legal team is going
           to spend time with you next and see how this needs
           to get sorted out. I just wanted to spend a few min-
           utes with you to let you know that things will move
           forward rather quickly from this point on.

Exec Suspect:
           Just a few more minutes, please. I need your help.

CEO: What do you think I can do for you?

Exec Suspect:
           I didn't do anything wrong.

CEO: That's not what the auditors think and it's not what
           I've been told.

Exec Suspect:
           They made a mistake. I don't know who told you
           what, but they aren't giving you the whole picture.

CEO: You're going to have to explain what's going on.

With an exchange like this, the relationship takes a critical turn. In the context of an interrogation, when Maddox lifts
the hood, the prisoner's main thought is, *Don't talk to this guy.*
That conviction has now shifted. He perceives that Maddox is
not only in a position to help him, but also that the interrogator

hasn't made up his mind about his guilt or innocence: "You have to convince the person you are shapeable. The source has to feel you don't want anything from him and that he can make an impression on you. When he believes that, he thinks, *Wait a second. I want to talk to this guy. It may not do any good, but it's the only shot I have at changing my circumstances.*"

The breakthrough in cultivating trust—that is, establishing rapport—occurs when the hostile source *wants* to talk to you. He feels the need for conversation as the only way to convince you to help him. Integral to having the trust take hold is to get the source to believe that you have the will and ability to follow through on doing some tough maneuvering to be helpful.

Having accomplished that, figuratively speaking, you try to get him to walk toward you—to want to be closer to you. In a situation where there is an enemy, you want him to come over to your side. Maddox often saw this happen with prisoners who saw that the American team was efficient and showed strength and precision in operations. They compared that to their own teams and decided they would be smart to switch allegiance to the United States.

In other situations with a hostile source, the shift might involve turning a state's witness or offering to gather information secretly that would be helpful to you. In the example of the senior executive, he might offer to cooperate so that others involved in the scheme would get caught.

It's reasonable to wonder if someone who decides to switch loyalties can be counted on to remain loyal and prove himself trustworthy. Maddox's anecdotal evidence is compelling. He's done more than 2,700 interrogations, but had only three prisoners dupe him after he'd determined they were being cooperative. He notes that, of course there were hundreds he did not get the cooperation of, but among those he felt he'd won over, almost all of them remained cooperative. It's an impressive conversion rate similar to that of Hans Scharff, who supposedly obtained salient information from 90 percent of the prisoners he interrogated.

Mentally Re-Orienting the Source

If you have ever gone to summer camp, boot camp, college, or any other immersive experience that lasted an extended period of time, then you can immediately grasp what happens in the next phase of the process. After your source cooperates, you try to get him into a completely different world. In a summer camp experience, the person leaves home and goes to a new environment; soon, he adapts to it and starts to feel comfortable in it. As long you can keep the person in the new environment, he will likely stay in it. In the business example, the CEO could move the senior executive to headquarters where he would have periodic access to her. A clandestine service officer would place his defector into a safe house where they could meet often and converse freely.

In some ways, this is like the military approach called "change of scene" that was described in Chapter 4. The big difference is that the approach is temporary; it's a matter of walking the source to the coffee machine instead of staying in the interrogation room the whole time. There is no sense of immersion, and though it might engender more open conversation, it wouldn't contribute to the kind of bonding that's the goal in this process.

In a war zone, an environment where the prisoner is removed from fighting and no longer has a constant concern about where to hide represents a completely different world. It doesn't have the elements of struggle that kept him on edge all the time. Maddox says, "It's like drug rehab for some people. You get them there and they are good with it. As long as they don't have to go back into society, they're fine."

Putting the Stakes Into Context

In television crime dramas, the detective commonly sits across a table from the accused murder and warns, "If eyewitnesses to the crime tell me you did it, you'll be on death row within three months." The CEO's version of this caution would be, "If our auditors prove you altered the books, you will pay a fine that's more than you could ever earn in a lifetime." In both cases, the success they had previously in drawing in their hostile source will evaporate.

What they've done is put the center of the discussion "out there" where the wrongdoing occurred. What they need to do is keep the focus "in here."

You aren't in a war zone. Even if you were, there are distinct advantages to keeping the discussion and the stakes of a transgression within the environment where the one-on-one interaction is occurring. You have a hostile source in front of you, who now has come to trust you on some level, so keep the conversation focused on what occurs in this context. Maddox provides a scenario that spotlights how this works:

Define the stakes in terms of what can happen inside the interrogation room, and shut out what others have said and threatened.

The prisoner probably says, "I'm innocent. I haven't done anything." But the set-up has to be that he feels it's beneficial to talk to me, even though he's been told that my team said he blew up Americans.

"No, no; ask me anything," he says. "I'll prove it to you that I'm innocent."

One approach that the training at Ft. Huachuca teaches would then have me say something like, "Okay, but if you killed people and I can prove it, then you go to prison for the rest of your life."

But I want to keep the focus on "in here" and not what he did "out there," so that's not what I would do. I'd say, "Listen, if I'm going to spend this time helping you, you cannot tell me a single lie."

The typical response is, "Mister, if I tell you a single lie, then you can kill me." This is a statement that he'd punctuate by running his finger across his neck like a knife slicing it.

I make it clear that I can't and wouldn't kill him, but if he told me a single lie, he would stay in this prison for the rest of his life. Then I juice it up; I give him good news: "But if you don't tell me a single lie, then I'll let you walk right out that door."

What just happened? I'm not having to prove what that guy did out there; I'm just having to catch him in a lie *in here.*

Put the stakes inside the interrogation booth. You can't prove what they did out there, but can catch them in a lie in the booth.

Questioning Well

Maddox cites questioning techniques as the single most valuable aspect of his interrogation training at Ft. Huachuca. It was what my coauthor Jim Pyle taught at the interrogation school and what we focused on in *Find Out Anything From Anyone, Anytime.* Specifically, Maddox sees value in differentiating between one type of question and another and in knowing how to use the different types in logical combination with each other to obtain the information being sought.

Even so, he puts his own spin on the execution. First, I'll clarify the types of questions (a more complete discussion is in Chapter 5) by citing examples related to prisoner interrogation and the CEO–senior executive scenario. After that, I'll cover Maddox's unique way of questioning and handling source leads.

Good questions

1. **Direct:** A straightforward question that opens with a basic interrogative word or phrase. The CEO asks the senior executive, "Did you alter the financial records?"

2. **Control:** A question for which you already have the answer. The CEO asks the executive, "How many direct reports do you have at that location?" even though he already knows that information.

3. **Repeat:** Two or more different questions that are after the same information. The CEO asks the executive, "When was the last time you accessed the financial records?" The executive responds, "March 30, at the end of the quarter." Toward the end of the conversation, which is taking place on May 15, she asks as she's going out the door, "By the way, I'm meeting with the board tomorrow and I need to tell them how many weeks it's been since you've accessed the financial records. What do I tell them?" Without thinking, the executive blurts out, "About two weeks."

4. **Persistent (or Follow-Up):** The same question, either reshaped a little or simply repeated to explore different angles of the desired information. A version of it is "What else?" So, an interrogator questioning a prisoner might ask

him what he was doing just prior to capture. The prisoner replies, "Eating lunch." The interrogator suspects that's not all he was doing, because the prisoner had a fresh cut on his leg, so he asks, "What else?"

5. **Summary:** An aid to revisiting an answer. The CEO says to the executive, "Do I understand you correctly that there were four people who had access to those records?" Just be careful and don't turn this into a compound question by trying to consolidate information. An example of this mistake is: "Do I understand you correctly that there were four people who had access to the information and that one of them was on maternity leave when the problems arose?"

6. **Non-Pertinent:** A question that ostensibly does not relate to the information you're seeking. In the discussion that follows, you will see how Maddox masterfully uses non-pertinent questions to arrive at pertinent information. A classic use of non-pertinent questions with a hostile source is to find out how he responds in a conversation that's relatively non-stressful because the topic has nothing to do with guilt or innocence.

Bad questions

1. **Leading:** The question supplies an answer. The CEO says to the executive prior to any guilt having been established, "How badly do you feel about manipulating the financial records?" The question should be a direct one at that stage: "Did you manipulate the records?"

2. **Negative:** Use of negative words such as "never" and "not" that confuse the point of the question. The interrogator says to the prisoner, "Are you not listening to me?"

3. **Vague:** A question lacking clarity, so the source may not
   be sure what information is being requested. The CEO
   asks the executive, "When you found out the auditors had
   entered the building and then they walked into your office
   unannounced with your assistant running behind them,
   what were you thinking?" The executive can pick and
   choose with this one, perhaps responding with, "I worried
   that someone had done something terrible to my assistant.
   She looked absolutely terrified." When you ask a vague
   question, if the source intends to hide the facts from you,
   this sets him up to hide them without even lying to you.

4. **Compound:** Posing two or more questions at one time. The
   interrogator asks the prisoner, "How did you get the bomb
   into the basement of that building and where did you get
   the materials to build it?"

>>>

Armed with his arsenal of different types of questions,
Maddox proceeds with an interrogation that more closely
resembles the kind of conversation you would have with someone you've just met on a long train ride. His combination of
all the good questions—direct, control, repeat, persistent,
summary, and non-pertinent—gives him a spectrum of information. He's particularly adept at showing how and why non-
pertinent questions can be a vital part of the exchange:

> If the prisoner is part of the insurgency, about 95 per-
> cent of his life is normal. He has a job and kids and
> a house to take care of. It's the other five percent of
> his time that's devoted to making bombs and planting
> IEDs. He will want to hide that five percent, but he
> will feel open about talking to me about that other 95
> percent of his existence. He'll open up in the hope that

I conclude that he's pretty clean. I ask about friends, family, job, relationship, travel, property, income and everything else. And somehow, I build a blueprint in my brain and from it, I can identify the hidden five percent.

Then I reveal that to the prisoner. You can see the look on his face; he knows he's been caught.

Maddox's summary of his questioning style doesn't capture the complexity of the process, which, to a great extent, depends on the way he follows source leads. If you were to go "by the book" (in the this case, that means following the Army Field Manual), then you would pick up a single source lead and follow it through. So, for example, if your source makes a reference to a friend he saw every day during the period of time when he was allegedly engaged in illegal activities, then you would go down a questioning path that focuses on the friend. In contrast, in the following example and explanation, Maddox illuminates how his process is different:

Let's say I'm talking to an Iraqi from Tikrit and our conversation is three or four hours. We start with questions about friends and family. While telling me about his family, he says he has three brothers—two older and one younger. He also has a couple of sisters. He has a farm. He likes to travel. He does a lot of things with his family.

I notice that when he's going to a wedding or other family gathering and he rides in a car, whenever he's with one or more of his brothers, his older brother drives. I'll ask, "Who did you ride with?"

"My oldest brother came up and picked us up."

Or he might say, "I drove over to my younger brother's house and picked him up."

So I get a picture of a certain dynamic. Whoever the older brother is in the scene, he's the one who drives. At some point, he tells me a story of going to a sister's wedding three years ago. He says his older brothers went in a different car and he was in the car with his younger brother. I ask, "Where were you sitting?"

He says, "In the back seat."

Suddenly, I'm missing an older sibling. I'll have to circle around in different ways to confirm that, but what I've done is build a picture in my head based upon data. But what I don't do is fill in any of the peripheral paint. Everything ties to data input.

Most people have a tendency to fill in the gaps through assumptions and perhaps through connecting dots that aren't there. I am not saying that I don't assume they were driving on a road, but it's not in my picture if the prisoner hasn't described it. I'm not going to ask a leading question like, "What happened when you drove down the road toward your mother's house?" That's filling in the paint in the picture. Don't plug in data you did not receive. But do use the data that you have.

I'm not labeling any of the information relevant or irrelevant. At the point when I get it, I just don't know. You must use what you have. Use *all* of what you have.

I'm not intuitive about this. I'm just a pragmatic person who collects data and sees how it fits and where the gaps are.

To explain more about Maddox's process, if he is trying to confirm that there's a missing sibling in a story, he has a suspicion that the prisoner is trying to hide something. It could be another family relationship, like a cousin. Or the source may talk freely about everyone in his family, but seems less inclined to be that open about his wife's younger brother. Or there might be a detail such as the prisoner saying he has one farm, but descriptions of terrain and buildings suggest that there are two. Or he said he went to Syria twice, but his narrative suggests he actually went three times.

Maddox doesn't ignore body language or tools like NLP (neuro-linguistic programming) as indicators of deception; however, he doesn't consider them primary. One physical cue that does stand out for him is a deviation in pace. If he's having a fluid conversation with the prisoner about his younger brother for three minutes and then his older brother for three minutes, and then there's halting conversation about the oldest brother, he will suspect that the source is trying to hide something. "But knowing that doesn't do much good," he says. "It's finding out what he's hiding that gets me where I need to go." He also needs to know why the source is hiding the information. Would he tell everyone this lie or just the American interrogator? You don't get that from reading body language, which merely indicates that stress is present and there's a likelihood that someone told a lie.

Maddox then works all of those pieces that seem to contain lies of omission into his questioning strategy. He says, "Those holes are part of the five percent of the prisoner's life that relates to his activities in the insurgency." Every question he then asks can build a confirmation of one or more of the missing pieces in the picture.

So the way he handles it is different from the standard map of following a source lead. There isn't just a missing brother. There's also a missing farm, a missing trip, and a missing brother-in-law, and he's working the leads simultaneously. The questions do "lean on" each other to gather more data for the picture, but it doesn't proceed in the straight path a student interrogator would see in the Army Field Manual.

The question for anyone without the natural mental agility of Eric Maddox is: How do you execute a strategy like this and follow multiple sources leads concurrently? It's so fundamental to his success that Maddox says unequivocally, "That's how I try to find the truth."

Maddox's technique sounds like a miracle of memory, but you may already be doing this to some extent without realizing it. His method is reminiscent of an approach that some respected journalists have used through the years. In the latter part of the 19th and early 20th centuries, William Henry Hills and Robert Luce, a journalist who later became a U.S. representative from Massachusetts, produced a series of volumes titled *The Writer.* In Volume 15, they advised:

> It is often a good rule for a reporter to get his whole story without taking a single note, and then go over it again with the person he is questioning, this time jotting down brief notes of names and important facts. Having "surrounded" the matter, so to speak, he knows what information he needs in the way of detail, and he can get it in proper order and to the best advantage.[2]

The man they cited as the original source of the advice was a renowned journalist name Charles Hemstreet, who first offered it in an 1866 book titled *The Reporter at Work.* Hemstreet's logic as expressed in that book tracks with how Maddox operates. Some people like Maddox—and I can personally relate to this—find note-taking distracting. We are better off listening to every word that someone says and then taking some time to process what we heard before asking follow-up questions and following source leads.

If this approach to questioning seems doable for you, then you will find yourself following multiple source leads at once. It will probably be useful to sort them mentally into people, places, things, and events so there is an underlying system of storing the leads—just as you would store them if you were taking physical notes.

Minimizing and Maximizing

Minimizing involves making your source feel less guilty or less wrong, and *maximizing* does the opposite. Used skillfully, both have value in extracting the truth from a hostile source, but these techniques aren't as simple to use as observing nervous gestures or avoiding bad questions. It's very easy to be clumsy with these techniques with the result being that your source knows you are manipulating what she perceives as the consequences of admitting to cheating, stealing, or any other transgression.

Minimizing

The following example illustrates a skillful use of minimizing because of where the interrogator places his emphasis.

As part of his work as a special agent in the Coast Guard Investigative Service, Michael Reilly had to interrogate a suspected child molester. He was actually beyond a suspect, as Reilly had ample evidence that the military officer seated before him had been having an incestuous relationship with his daughter. The last thing that Reilly—himself the father of young daughters—wanted to do was build rapport with a heinous predator. But he knew he had to do it in order to get a confession. Without a confession to avert a trial, the girl's nightmares would be fueled by the drama in a courtroom where she would be asked to tell a room full of strangers what her father had done. So Reilly began building a bridge, father to father.

They talked about the challenges of being a father to a beautiful daughter. They would do anything for their daughters, they agreed, even though sometimes it was painful to them. Reilly wanted his suspect to feel as though he understood him; he wanted the man to get the sense that his actions regarding his daughter were acceptable, even normal. He steadily moved toward the conversational territory where he could bring up the subject of sexual relations, eventually suggesting that he understood how a father might want to teach his daughter about being with a man so her first experience would be with someone who loved her, someone who would have sex with her to protect her from harsh surprises later on.

As the man began to trust Reilly, he talked about how he had done just that. He stuck with the approach to minimizing that Reilly had established, saying things like "I was trying to teach my daughter the ways of the world. I didn't want her to learn it from a stranger."

Reilly's emphasis was on assuming a friendly demeanor, expressing understanding and even sympathy, boosting the man's ego by suggesting he did something wise, and ultimately touching his conscience. It's what researchers in the field of interrogation strategies call a "no consequences" approach to minimizing.

In contrast, a "consequences" approach would specifically downplay the consequences of the transgression and stress the benefits, in terms of leniency, of cooperating with the interrogator. Studies have shown that the consequences style of minimizing has a greater chance of eliciting a false confession or other incorrect information than Reilly's no-consequences use of the technique.[3]

Maximizing

In Chapter 4, I briefly referenced military-style conversation motivators, otherwise known to interrogators as
"approaches." Some of them are key elements in the maximizing technique, which is more confrontational in nature than
minimizing. These elements might include the we-know-all
and fear-up (mild) approaches. So, for example, you might
confront your cheating spouse by saying that you've seen the
text messages from his mistress—even though you haven't, but
you know he texts a lot—and that you intend to tell his mother,
who would likely disinherit him for his adultery because of her
religious beliefs.

The holes in adopting this technique are probably obvious.
Anytime you assert absolutely certainty about someone's guilt,
if you don't have hard evidence of that guilt, the ice underneath
you is thin. And nearly anytime you integrate a third party into
the scenario, you have introduced a significant variable.

A better way to maximize would be simply to assume an
unfriendly demeanor and assert a firm belief in guilt.[4] This is
the no-consequences style of maximizing that is more likely to
provoke truthfulness and less likely to aggravate the source to
the point of outrage, anger, and denial.

>>>

The fundamental premise of any technique designed
to lure a hostile source into telling the truth is this: You are
dealing with a human being. Human beings, unless they are
aberrant, want to feel connected to others. The techniques
described throughout this book are interpersonal skills that
allow you to connect with others effectively and exploit that
connection through conversation.

You *can* fool yourself, you know. You'd think it's
impossible, but it turns out it's the easiest thing of all.[1]

—Jodi Picoult, author

Self-assessment may be the most consistently useful application of all the skills. Your relationships, health, and career
depend on giving yourself nothing but the truth.

Actually, that may or may not be true all the time. Perhaps
there are times when deceiving yourself is useful.

This chapter delves into circumstances in which telling
yourself the truth is vital to your well-being and how you can
nurture that, as well as when a bit of self-deception might be
adventageous.

Relationships

While collecting insights from experts and personal stories
for this book, I received an e-mail from someone I've never
met. A close associate of mine asked her to contribute her story
as a way of illustrating how a very bright woman (her graduate degree is from Harvard) failed to do the self-examination

that could have spared her grief and expense. The name in the e-mail has been changed to protect the contributor's identity:

> My ex left on January 1, 2009. My stepdaughter called a week later to say he was living at a woman's house. He had told me he was staying with an "investor" to sort out his feelings.
>
> I couldn't take it in until 6 weeks later, Hilary called again to tell me he really was with her. He did marry her (briefly) after the divorce and of course after spending a ton of her money. I truly could NOT believe he was cheating.
>
> I still have trouble with taking in that he was lying and cheating. In June I got sued by an ex-partner of his because my ex forged my signature on a personal guarantee for $1.3 million. (Delightful to be shelling out a sick amount of money to defend myself.)
>
> I can't believe I am still shocked!!

From my coauthoring ventures with family and couples' therapist Trevor Crow, I knew she had heard many stories similar to this one and guided people toward healing with *emotionally focused therapy (EFT)*. Her advice on how to begin being truthful with yourself about someone whose trustworthiness you question doesn't begin with a cognitive experience. That is, she doesn't recommend poking your psyche with logical questions, creating checklists of pros and cons related to the person, or writing down all the facts of the matter and analyzing them. Her advice is more compassionate: Try a *somatic experience.* In a somatic experience, you focus on your body sensations as a way of getting in touch more honestly with your thoughts and emotions about a person, place, thing, or event in time. To understand what it feels like, she advises:

Sit still next to another person. Pay careful attention to the way your body reacts to this person close to you.

Is your physical experience one of calm and softness? A feeling of safety and well-being? Or is it a gut feeling of tenseness, perhaps excitement? Is there a feeling of not knowing? Maybe a little off balance?

Listen carefully to your gut feelings and pay attention to your intuition. Your physical experience won't lie to you.[2]

Once you understand the sensations of a somatic experience, try it with the person whose trustworthiness you question. You will respond on a physiological level. Remember all those signs of stress described in earlier parts of the book, such as suddenly noticing adaptors and barriers, or changes in posture? They aren't just things that other people do. Monitor your own deviations from baseline to see if you are showing signs of stress.

After you've determined how you *feel,* then pull away and take some time to figure out how you *think.* In other words, lead with your authentic responses to being near the person and follow up with good questions to yourself.

Health

When we feel ill or uncomfortable, the voice inside usually asks: "What is this?" "What's causing this?" "How did this happen?" The first response that another voice inside our head gives is often the product of rationalizing. Answers might include: "It's nothing; it will go away," "It's probably the weather causing it," or "I must have bumped into something without realizing it."

For some people, self-deception about a health issue is not just making up excuses as to why we have symptoms. It is a

mental illness called *anosognosia,* the medical term for not seeing what ails you. Rather than simple psychological denial—and
most of us can relate to that—people who suffer from this condition will even deny something as obvious and serious as paralysis.

The rest of us are just engaging in the destructive diversion
called rationalizing. But when it comes to our health, we want
accurate answers as soon as possible.

To illustrate both the value and mechanism of questioning
for self-assessment, let's begin with a true story. In spring 2013,
the discomfort a client of mine had in one hip became pain in
both hips, weakness and pain in the hip flexors, and occasional
lower back pain. She received multiple diagnoses from different
practitioners, none of whom thought that an MRI or x-rays would
be necessary. She also went through numerous therapies, but the
relief she got was short-lived—anywhere from a few minutes to
roughly half an hour. Some of the therapies had no effect at all.

The chronic, debilitating symptoms made it painful and
difficult to do anything that involved lifting her legs, from walking, to putting on pants, to going up and down stairs. Everyone
around her thought the problems must have something to do
with her athletic background. After all, how could she be normal after years of intense competition in sports such as gym-
nastics, bodybuilding, powerlifting, and adventure races of 400
miles in length? Medical professionals added that her current,
largely sedentary, posture during the day while designing had
an important role in exacerbating the symptoms.

And then I introduced her to ultra-endurance athlete and
World Record holder "Epic" Bill Bradley. He didn't focus on
her symptoms the way other athletes and medical professionals
did. He asked her the question that a good questioner asks—and
one that she had neglected to ask herself: "What *else* could be

causing this?" She couldn't even speculate, never even having asked the question. Rather than try to guide her toward other answers, he recommended a book called *Healing Back Pain,* first published in 1991. The author, Dr. John E. Sarno, is professor of clinical rehabilitation medicine at New York University School of Medicine, and attending physician at the Howard A. Rusk Institute of Rehabilitation Medicine, New York University Medical Center. His premise is that a person's response to tension can cause real, physical disorders such as those she was experiencing. "Epic" Bill credits that book with helping him recover completely from serious back pain that had persisted for 14 months; his recovery was a gateway occurrence to a series of astonishing endurance feats.

Through the book, it seemed to her and to me as though Sarno continued the good questioning that Bill had begun. Over a two-week period, thoughts about what else was causing this started to take shape in her head. She linked the onset of the physical symptoms with the most intense period of deadlines and demands in her professional life.

Then her own good questioning began: *What, or who, is making me chronically tense and/or angry? What would happen if I didn't assume there would be pain? What would happen if I tried harder to work through it?* She gave herself honest answers; the pain remained, but it varied in terms of intensity and location. With Sarno's voice in her head, she kept asking the questions on a daily basis and finally gave herself the truth: She felt huge, unrelenting pressure to perform as a designer. She even felt guilty reading a novel at bedtime because she wasn't being "productive."

One day some weeks after that, she got out of her car at the grocery store. As she walked toward the door, she realized she had no pain. Walking through the aisles, she had no pain. When she got home, she went up and down the stairs. She experienced discomfort and weakness, but no pain. The next day was about the same, so she tried a few exercises that were somewhat more vigorous than what she'd done in the past. But then the pain returned.

She began physical therapy with someone who made the connection between her chronic problems and stress. After a few sessions, she was climbing stairs, walking briskly, doing light weight-training, and handling daily tasks with relative ease.

The truth: She was stressed out beyond anything she had experienced before but was unwilling to admit it. Not recognizing that truth had both exacerbated minor physical problems and triggered new ones. These problems constricted her movement, her health, and her enjoyment of life. When she stopped kidding herself, she started healing.

Career

Tom followed in his father's footsteps and sold life insurance for a living. He had a wife, two young daughters, and a stepson in college, all of whom depended on his impressive income. The self-deception that pervaded his life was that his high performance as an insurance salesman meant that he was a good match for the career. When he was just about to turn 50, he told his wife that what he really wanted to do was make sandwiches.

She attributed the remark to his bizarre sense of humor—the one that she wished he had "left in Boston." Then Tom told her that he wanted to work out a plan with her to open a small deli at the start of tourist season in their small town and see if he could make a go of actually making sandwiches. He was a naturally gifted cook who had concocted 10 unusual sandwiches and a couple of soups.

He opened the deli and it was a hit—for the five months of the year that tourists were in town. Other than that, his life was a struggle, but he remained happy and optimistic, and he earned enough through catering parties during the off-season to keep his family in their beautiful home.

By the time Tom contracted a life-threatening illness and had to give up his deli, he had spent 10 happy years making sandwiches. The truth was, it was what he was meant to do.

Clarity about what you want to do with your life can be hard to come by—not as obvious as Tom's passion to make sandwiches. It's particularly difficult if you're very good at something that pays well and is at least marginally satisfying. Having spent more than a decade doing marketing communications in the high-tech industry, I knew the story of achievement, financial reward, and complacency very well. But I was lucky: I got a kick in the psyche in the form of a layoff.

Feeling a little dazed and confused, I attended an Anthony Robbins seminar. Somewhere in the middle of it, I heard him ask the question, "Where do you see yourself in five years?" I *really* heard the question. And the answer came down to an internal battle between certainty and uncertainty. I could either safely splash in the kiddie pool and lie to myself that life was grand, or finally dive off the high board and face a high-risk truth: I wanted to write for a living.

So the answer was this: In five years, I see myself signing copies of my new book.

Just as your emotions serve you well in ascertaining the truth of your relationships, they will serve you well in finding it in your career. It's important to know what you're good at doing, but ask yourself which of those things you're good at energizes you emotionally.

For *Psychology Today,* author Kat McGowan researched the topic of self-deception and profiled four people who triumphed over it in her article "Living a Lie." Her conclusion, which should provide some comfort to all of us, is this:

> There is no particular personality type that is more vulnerable to self-deception. We are all equally susceptible, especially when anxiety gets the better of us. In general, accepting our flaws alongside our strengths provides a bulwark against excessive self-deception; so does coming to peace with our own internal contradictions and learning to withstand difficult feelings, such as doubt and fear.[3]

Benefits of Lying to Yourself

It may seem odd to end a book on truth detection with a section on the value of lying to yourself. My rationale is that realizing the truth of what you want to accomplish in life and how you want to feel may benefit from a bit of self-deception. In other words, there's a bigger truth at stake for you.

Joanna Starek, currently a senior partner with the management consulting firm RHR International, is a PhD psychologist who has worked as a performance enhancement consultant with elite athletes. She defines self-deception as follows: "Self-deception is that you have two contradictory beliefs and you hold them at the same time. You allow one of them into conscious, and you have a motivation for allowing one of them into consciousness."[4]

People do this all the time with relationships. You allow your truth to be "He loves me and wants to be with me" even though you know that he's apartment hunting and is moving out imminently. Or you allow "She's faithful to me," even though you've seen the e-mails documenting her rendezvous with a man from work. Your motivation is that you want the thought to be true so you'll treat it as though it is.

Unfortunately, that type of self-deception is not useful, and neither is lying to yourself about the possibility of being fired at work or the need to address certain medical symptoms. However, Starek conducted a study that suggests that self-deception can have positive effects—that allowing a thought that isn't true, or isn't true *yet,* to take shape *as* truth in the conscious mind. The genesis of her study was an interest in finding an answer to "How can you have two people have the same physiological capacity, yet one consistently outperforms the other?"

She administered a test designed in the 1970s by two psychiatrists, Harold Sackheim and Ruben Gur, that features embarrassing questions that provoke two contradictory answers: yes or no. Through the years, some researchers have administered a later version of the questionnaire requesting a 1–7 response to indicate answers ranging from "not at all" to "very much so." Some of the questions are[5]:

▸ Have you ever felt hatred toward either of your parents?

▸ Have you ever felt like you wanted to kill somebody?

▸ Have you ever doubted your sexual adequacy?

▸ Have you ever enjoyed your bowel movements?

▸ Have you ever thought of committing suicide in order to get back at someone?

The underlying assertion is that people are lying to themselves when they give a negative response to the questions—that everyone has, at some point, thought or felt these things.

In Starek's study, she and her research partner gave the questionnaire at the beginning of the season to the swim team at Colgate University, which has a long history of highly competitive swimmers. They trained throughout the season to qualify for the Eastern Athletic Conference Championship. "It's a very objective measure," notes Starek. "You either swim fast enough during the season to qualify or you don't."[6]

At the end of the season, Starek found what she calls "a bizarre relationship." The athletes who had answered no to the embarrassing questions did much better: "Consistently, they were the winners."[7] So, the fastest and most successful swimmers were the ones who had lied to themselves.

In more than sports, denying certain facts about the real world around you—according to any number of new studies—produces people who, it turns out, are better at business and better at working with teams. And here's the real kicker: They turn out to be happier people.[8]

People who are most realistic, seeing the world exactly as it is, tend to be more depressed than their counterparts, who engage in some self-deception. They are honest about pain they've caused others, are realistic about their shortcomings, and face the brutal facts of the harshness and brutality in the world.

Those people who do not deceive themselves are right in the sense they are truthful. But we are all vulnerable, and sometimes, telling ourselves a better story than the one that is true is part of how we cope.

Jean-Paul Sartre would not agree with that latter assertion, of course. The famous 20th-century philosopher and author firmly believed that self-deception is "an immediate, permanent threat to every project of the human being."[9] But Sartre was a philosopher, which few of us are. For those of us whose thoughts are less lofty and our emotions more dominant, it might better to allow ourselves an occasional bout of self-deception.

Chapter Notes

Chapter 1

1. Eric Maddox, interview with the author, May 1, 2014.
2. "Eyewitness Misidentification." The Innocence Project Website. *www.innocenceproject.org/understand/Eyewitness-Misidentification.php.*
3. "How Many Senses Does a Human Being Have?" HowStuffWorks Website. *http://science.howstuffworks.com/life/question242.htm.*
4. Michael Kimmelman, "ART; Absolutely Real? Absolutely Fake?" *The New York Times,* August 4, 1991.
5. Malcolm Gladwell, *Blink: The Power of Thinking Without Thinking* (Little, Brown & Company, 2005), Introduction.
6. Ibid, p. 8.
7. Herbert Spiegel, MD, and David Spiegel, MD, *Trance and Treatment,* Second Edition (American Psychiatric Publishing, 2004), p. 113.
8. J. Eric Oliver and Thomas J. Wood, "Conspiracy Theories and the Paranoid Style(s) of Mass Opinion," *American Journal of Political Science,* first published online March 5, 2014, DOI: 10.1111/ajps.12084.

9. Shankar Vedantam, "More Americans Than You Might Think Believe in Conspiracy Theories," Morning Edition, National Public Radio, June 4, 2014, *www.npr.org/2014/06/04/318733298/more-americans-than-you-might-think-believe-in-conspiracy-theories.*

10. David Major, retired senior FBI supervisory special agent and first director of Counterintelligence, Intelligence and Security Programs at the National Security Council at the White House, interview with the author, June 2, 2014.

11. Art Swift, "Majority in U.S. Still Believe JFK Killed in a Conspiracy," Gallup Politics, November 15, 2013, *www.gallup.com/poll/165893/majority-believe-jfk-killed-conspiracy.aspx.*

12. Retired Major General Oleg Kalugin, formerly deputy chief of the KGB residency in Washington, DC, interview, June 22, 2014.

13. David Major, retired senior FBI supervisory special agent and first director of Counterintelligence, Intelligence and Security Programs at the National Security Council at the White House, interview with the author, June 2, 2014.

14. Boghardt, Thomas. "Active Measures: The Russian Art of Disinformation." International Spy Museum Website. *www.spymuseum.org/education-programs/spy-resources/background-briefings/active-measures/.*

15. Shankar Vedantam, "More Americans Than You Might Think Believe in Conspiracy Theories," Morning Edition, National Public Radio, June 4, 2014, *www.npr.org/2014/06/04/318733298/more-americans-than-you-might-think-believe-in-conspiracy-theories.*

16. Will Gervais and Ara Norenzayan, "Analytic Thinking Promotes Religious Disbelief," *Science* 336, 493 (2012), DOI: 10.1126/science.1215647, and *www.sciencedaily.com/releases/2012/04/120426143856.htm.*

17. Sam Harris, Jonas Kaplan, Ashley Curiel, Susan Y. Bookheimer, Marco Iacoboni, and Mark S. Cohen, "The

Neural Correlates of Religious and Nonreligious Belief," University of California, Los Angeles, October 1, 2009, DOI: 10.137/journal.pone.0007272, *www.plosone.org/ article/info%3Adoi%2F10.1371%2Fjournal.pone.0007272* .

18. Wendy R. Aronsson, LCSW, interview with the author, April 20, 2014.

19. Trevor Crow and Maryann Karinch, *Forging Health Connections: How Relationships Fight Illness, Aging and Depression* (New Horizon Press, 2013), p. 108.

Chapter 2

1. Brian Williams extended interview with Edward Snowden, NBC Nightly News, May 28, 2014, *www.nbcnews.com/ feature/edward-snowden-interview/exclusive-edward-snowden-tells-brian-williams-i-was-trained-spy-n115746.*

2. Dylan Matthews, "Fact-Checking Obama's Speech," *The Washington Post,* September 7, 2012, *www.washingtonpost. com/blogs/wonkblog/wp/2012/09/07/fact-checking-obamas-speech/.*

3. PolitiFact.com Website, *www.politifact.com.*

4. "Barack Obama Says, 'We've Doubled Our Use of Renewable Energy'," Politifact.com Website, *www. politifact.com/truth-o-meter/statements/2012/sep/11/ barack-obama/barack-obama-says-weve-doubled-our-use-renewable-e/.*

5. Ibid.

6. Retired Major General Oleg Kalugin, formerly deputy chief of the KGB residency in Washington, DC, interview with the author, June 22, 2014.

7. Jack Devine, *Good Hunting* (Sarah Crichton, 2014), pp 47–48.

8. David Major, retired senior FBI supervisory special agent and first director of Counterintelligence, Intelligence and Security Programs at the National Security Council at the White House, interview with the author, June 2, 2014.

9. "Looking Back at Lance Armstrong's Many Denials,"
    Associated Press video, YouTube.com Website, *www.
    youtube.com/watch?v=4RBjrLGdw7c.*

10. Jack Devine, interview with the author, May 29, 2014.

11. Glenn Kessler, "Do Nine out of 10 New Businesses Fail,
    as Rand Paul Claims?" Fact Checker, *The Washington
    Post,* January 27, 2014, *www.washingtonpost.com/blogs/fact-
    checker/wp/2014/01/27/do-9-out-of-10-new-businesses-fail-
    as-rand-paul-claims/.*

12. Richard Sheldrake, "Richard Dawkins Comes to Call" as
    quoted by Deepak Chopra in "I Know I'm Right, So Why
    Be Fair?" *The Huffington Post,* January 11, 2008, *www.
    huffingtonpost.com/deepak-chopra/i-know-im-right-so-why-
    be_b_81095.html.*

13. Ibid.

14. Ibid.

15. William James, *Principles of Psychology,* pp. 193–195.

16. Lena Sisco, interview with the author, April 14, 2014.

17. Paul Ekman, *Telling Lies: Clues to Deceit in the Market
    Place, Marriage, and Politics,* Third Edition (Norton,
    2001).

18. Marc Mehu, et al., "Reliable Facial Muscle Activation
    Enhances Recognizability and Credibility of Emotional
    Expression," *Emotion* Vol. 12, No. 4 (2012): 701–715,
    American Psychological Association

19. Michael B. Kelley, "Body-Language Expert: I Would Not
    Trust Anything Snowden Said to NBC," *Business Insider,*
    May 30, 2014, *www.businessinsider.com/body-language-
    expert-analyzes-snowdens-nbc-interview-2014-5.*

20. Janine Driver on Today, March 31, 2014, *www.today.com/
    video/today/54826647#54826647.*

21. Ibid.

Chapter 3
1. Elizabeth Bancroft, interview with the author, April 27, 2014.
2. E. Peter Earnest, interview with the author, June 2, 2014.
3. Louis Tay and Ed Deiner, "Needs and Subjective Well-Being Around the World," *Journal of Personality and Social Psychology* Vol. 101, No. 2 (2011): 354–365, DOI: 10.1037/a0023779, *http://academic.udayton.edu/jackbauer/Readings%20595/Tay%20Diener%2011%20needs%20WB%20world%20copy.pdf*.
4. "The WWII Interrogator Who Used Kindness Over Violence," BBC, October 15, 2012, *www.bbc.co.uk/history/0/19923902*.
5. Lena Sisco, interview with the author, April 14, 2014.
6. Ibid.
7. Amy Cuddy, "Your Body Language Shapes Who You Are," TEDGlobal, filmed June 2012, *www.ted.com/talks/amy_cuddy_your_body_language_shapes_who_you_are*.
8. Ibid.
9. Ibid.
10. Peter A. Andersen, *Nonverbal Communication: Forms and Functions* (McGraw-Hill, 1998).
11. Lena Sisco, interview with the author, April 14, 2014.
12. Michael Reilly, interview with the author, April 5, 2014.
13. Ibid.
14. Julio Viskovich, "How to Build Rapport Quickly," LinkedIn, April 21, 2014, *www.linkedin.com/today/post/article/20140421142434-14028329-how-to-build-rapport-quickly*.
15. "Joining Freemasonry," Anti-Masonry Points of View Website, *www.masonicinfo.com/member.htm*.

16. Stephanie Tom Tong, Brandon Van Der Heide, Lindsey
Langwell, and Joseph B. Walther, "Too Much of a Good
Thing? The Relationship Between Number of Friends
and Interpersonal Impressions on Facebook," *Journal of
Computer-Mediated Communication* Volume 13, Issue
3 (April 2008): 531–549, *http://onlinelibrary.wiley.com/
doi/10.1111/j.1083-6101.2008.00409.x/full#ss13*.

17. Ibid.

18. Benjamin Weiser, *A Secret Life: The Polish Officer, His
Covert Mission, and the Price He Paid to Save His Country*
(Public Affairs, 2004), pp. 88–89.

Chapter 4

1. E. Peter Earnest, interview with the author, June 2, 2014.

2. Including some paraphrasing of FM 34–52, pp. 3–14 to
3–20.

3. George Loewenstein, "The Psychology of Curiosity: A
Review and Reinterpretation," *Psychological Bulletin* Vol.
116, No. 1 (1994): 75–98, *www.cmu.edu/dietrich/sds/docs/
loewenstein/PsychofCuriosity.pdf.*

4. "Study: Brian Battles Itself Over Short-Term Rewards,
Long-Term Goals," Princeton University press release,
October 14, 2004, *www.princeton.edu/pr/news/04/q4/1014-
brain.htm.*

5. George Loewenstein, "The Psychology of Curiosity: A
Review and Reinterpretation," *Psychological Bulletin* Vol.
116, No. 1 (1994): 75–98, *www.cmu.edu/dietrich/sds/docs/
loewenstein/PsychofCuriosity.pdf.*

6. Aaron Ben-Zeév, "Are Negative Emotions More
Important Than Positive Emotions?" PsychologyToday.
com, July 18, 2010, *www.psychologytoday.com/blog/in-the-
name-love/201007/are-negative-emotions-more-important-
positive-emotions.*

7. Ibid.

8. Diana Fosha, Daniel J. Siegel, and Marion F. Solomon (Eds.), *The Healing Power of Emotion* (W.W. Norton, 2009), which contains articles by Siegel and Schore.

9. Piercarlo Valdesolo, "Flattery Will Get You Far," *Scientific American,* January 12, 2010, *www. scientificamerican.com/article/flattery-will-get-you-far/.*

10. Ibid.

11. Dov Cohen, Richard E. Nisbett, Brian F. Bowdle, and Norbert Schwartz, "Insult, Aggression, and the Southern Culture of Honor: An 'Experimental Ethnography,'" *Journal of Personality and Social Psychology* Vol. 70, No. 5 (May 1996): 945–960, *http://mypages.valdosta.edu/ mwhatley/7670/activity/honor.htm.*

12. Jean M. Twenge, Roy F. Baumeister, C. Nathan DeWall, Natalie J.Ciarocco, and J. Michael Bartels, "Social Exclusion Decreases Prosocial Behavior," *Journal of Personality and Social Psychology* Vol. 92, No. 1 (2007): 56–66.

13. Ibid.

14. Eric Maddox, *Mission: Black List #1* (Harper, 2008), p. 229.

15. Ibid.

16. Ibid, p. 227.

17. Jim McCormick, interview with the author, July 11, 2014.

18. Kris Kosaka, "Professor Finds Meaning in Silence," *The Japan Times,* October 16, 2010.

19. Bruce Fell, "Bring the Noise: Has Technology Made Us Scared of Silence?" *The Conversation,* December 30, 2012, *http://theconversation.com/bring-the-noise-has-technology-made-us-scared-of-silence-10988.*

20. "John Cage - 4'33"," YouTube.com, *www.youtube.com/ watch?v=zY7UK-6aaNA.*

21. FM 32–52, p. 3–13.

Chapter 5

1. Terry Gross interviewing Joaquin Phoenix, Fresh Air, WHYY/National Public Radio, January 21, 2014, *www.npr.org/templates/transcript/transcript. php?storyId=264524233.*

2. "Bill O'Reilly Angry At Barney Frank (10-2-08)," YouTube.com, *www.youtube.com/watch?v=Unj-kcGOe5I.*

3. Jeremy Hobson, e-mail to the author, May 22, 2014.

4. Jeremy Hobson, interview with the author, April 25, 2014.

Chapter 6

1. Jack Devine, interview with the author, May 29, 2014.

2. Ray Decker, interview with the author, July 18, 2014.

3. Nicholas D. Kristof, "Why Didn't We Stop 9/11?" *The New York Times,* April 17, 2004, *www.nytimes.com/2004/04/17/ opinion/why-didn-t-we-stop-9-11.html.*

4. "9/11 Was Foreseeable," Washington's Blog Website, April 26, 2008, *www.washingtonsblog.com/2008/04/911-was-foreseeable.html.*

5. Charles Seife, *Virtual Unreality: Just Because the Internet Told You, How Do You Know It's True?* (Viking Adult, 2014).

6. Ibid.

7. Jack Devine, interview with the author, May 29, 2014.

8. Ira Flatow's interview with Charles Seife, "A Web of Doubt," Public Radio International's Science Friday, July 4, 2014.

9. Leo Sun, "Twitter's Very Real Fake Problem," The Motley Fool Website, April 15, 2014, *www.fool.com/investing/ general/2014/04/15/twitters-very-real-fake-problem.aspx.*

10. Ibid.

11. Heather Kelly, "83 Million Facebook Accounts Are Fakes and Dupes," CNN.com, August 2, 2012, *www.cnn. com/2012/08/02/tech/social-media/facebook-fake-accounts/.*

12. Ryan Holiday, e-mail to the author, July 15, 2014.

13. Roberta Wohlstetter, *Pearl Harbor: Warning and Decision* (Stanford University Press, 1962).

14. Ray Decker, interview with the author, June 2, 2014.

15. Ibid.

16. Ray Decker, interview with the author, July 18, 2014.

17. Deborah Schroeder-Saulnier, *The Power of Paradox* (Career Press, 2014), p. 126.

18. Jack Devine, interview with the author, May 29, 2014.

19. Ibid.

20. Mark Lowenthal, "What Is Intelligence?" from "Lesson 7: The Intelligence Process, Foundations of Geographic Information and Spatial Analysis," Pennsylvania State University College of Earth and Mineral Sciences, *https:// courseware.e-education.psu.edu/courses/bootcamp/lo07/04. html.*

Chapter 7

1. M.F. Mendez and I.A. Fras, "The False Memory Syndrome: Experimental Studies and Comparison to Confabulations," *Medical Hypotheses* 76(4) (April 2011): 492–496, *www.ncbi.nlm.nih.gov/pmc/articles/PMC3143501/.*

2. Dr. Jeremy Dean, "How Memories Are Distorted and Invented: Misattribution," PsyBlog, *www.spring.org. uk/2008/02/how-memories-are-distorted-and-invented.php.*

3. D.L. Schacter, J.L. Harbluk, and D.R. McLachlan, "Retrieval Without Recollection: An Experimental Analysis of Source Amnesia," *Journal of Verbal Learning and Verbal Behavior* 23 (1984): 593–611.

4. Lyn Goff and Henry Roediger, "Imagination Inflation for Action Events: Repeated Imaginings Lead to Illusory Recollections," *Memory & Cognition* 26 (1998): 20–33, *http://psych.wustl.edu/memory/Roddy%20article%20PDF's/ Goff%20&%20Roediger%20(1998)_MemCog.pdf.*

5. Siri Carpenter citing Richard L. Marsh, "Plagiarism or Memory Glitch?" *Monitor,* American Psychological Association, Vol. 33, No. 2 (February 2002), p. 25, *www. apa.org/monitor/feb02/glitch.aspx.*

6. Ibid.

7. Ibid.

8. Ian Stevenson, "Cryptomnesia and Parapsychology," lecture delivered March 19, 1982, London, *www.medicine. virginia.edu/clinical/departments/psychiatry/sections/cspp/ dops/dr.-stevensons-publications/STE11Stevenson%201983. pdf.*

9. Daniel L. Schacter, *Searching for Memory: The Brain, the Mind, and the Past* (Basic Books, 1997).

10. From a 1999 interview with Brian Boitano for *Lessons From the Edge* (Simon & Schuster/Fireside, 2000), p. 51.

11. M.F. Mendez and I.A. Fras, "The False Memory Syndrome: Experimental Studies and Comparison to Confabulations," *Medical Hypotheses* 76(4) (April 2011): 492–496, *www.ncbi.nlm.nih.gov/pmc/articles/PMC3143501/.*

12. Harvey Austin, MD, interview with the author, July 15, 2014.

13. Ibid.

14. Ibid.

15. Sue Rotolo, interview with the author, August 14, 2014.

16. M.P. Koss, S. Tromp, and M. Tharan, "Traumatic Memories: Empirical Foundations, Forensic and Clinical Implications," *Clinical Psychology: Science and Practice* 2 (2) (1995): 111–132.

17. Sue Rotolo, interview with the author, August 14, 2014.

18. Ibid.

19. Ibid.

20. "Building Trust With Cooperative Witnesses in a Crime Investigation," article on the Science Daily Website, March 1, 2011, profiling results of a study done by Jonathan P. Vallano, published in *Applied Cognitive Psychology* (March 2011), *www.sciencedaily.com/releases/2011/03/110301122227.htm.*

21. Jonathan P. Vallano and Nadja Schriber Compo, "A Comfortable Witness Is a Good Witness: Rapport-Building and Susceptibility to Misinformation in an Investigative Mock-Crime Interview," *Applied Cognitive Psychology* (2011), DOI: 10, 1002/acp. 1789.

22. Ibid.

23. Ronald P. Fisher and R. Edward Geiselman, "The Cognitive Interview Method of Conducting Police Interviews: Eliciting Extensive Information and Promoting Therapeutic Jurisprudence," *International Journal of Law and Psychiatry* 33 (2010): 321–328, *www.how2ask.nl/wp-content/uploads/2013/08/Fisher_2010_International-Journal-of-Law-and-Psychiatry.pdf.*

24. Ibid.

25. Dean Hohl and Maryann Karinch, *Rangers Lead the Way: The Army Rangers' Guide to Leading Your Organization Through Chaos* (Adams Media, 2003), pp. 170–171.

Chapter 8

1. David Major, retired senior FBI supervisory special agent and first director of Counterintelligence, Intelligence and Security Programs at the National Security Council at the White House, interview with the author, June 2, 2014.

2. Peter Earnest and Maryann Karinch, *Business Confidential* (AMACOM Books, 2001), p. 170.

3. T. Evan Schaeffer, *Deposition Checklists and Strategies* (James Publishing, 2012), pp. 1–34.

4. "GPO Nara Part 1: Nixon's Grand Jury Testimony Taken on June 23, 1975," available online at *www.scribd.com/doc/72357126/GPO-Nara-Part-1-Nixon-s-grand-jury-testimony-taken-on-June-23-1975.*

5. Ibid.

6. Ibid.

7. Ibid.

8. "Armstrong Denies New Doping Allegations," Associated Press video, YouTube.com, *www.youtube.com/watch?v=mSwStl7X--4.*

9. "Deception," Radiolab, Season 4, Episode 2, *www.radiolab.org/story/91612-deception/.*

10. "Dynamic Facial Expressions of Emotion Transmit Hierarchical Information Over Time," Rachael E. Jack, Institute of Neuroscience and Psychology, University of Glasgow, Glasgow, Scotland, January 14, 2014, available online at *www.youtube.com/watch?v=HNWMO7GkgOk.*

11. Aleix Martinez, Shichuan Du, "A Model of the Perception of Facial Expressions of Emotion by Humans: Research Overview and Perspectives," *Journal of Machine Learning Research* 13 (2012): 1589–1609, *http://jmlr.org/papers/volume13/martinez12a/martinez12a.pdf.*

12. Rachael E. Jack, Oliver G.B. Garrod, and Philippe G. Schyns, "Dynamic Facial Expressions of Emotion Transmit an Evolving Hierarchy of Signals Over Time," *Current Biology* (2014): 5, *http://dx.doi.org/10.1016/j.cub.2013.11.064.*

13. Lena Sisco, interview with the author, April 14, 2014.

14. David Major, retired senior FBI supervisory special agent and first director of Counterintelligence, Intelligence and Security Programs at the National Security Council at the White House, interview with the author, June 2, 2014.

15. Yaling Yang, et al., "Localisation of Increased Prefrontal White Matter in Pathological Liars," *British Journal of Psychiatry* 190 (February 2007): 174–175, *www.ncbi.nlm. nih.gov/pmc/articles/PMC2376803/*.

Chapter 9

1. Eric Maddox, interview with the author, May 1, 2014. All subsequent quotes from Maddox in this chapter are also taken from this interview.
2. William Henry Hills and Robert Luce, *The Writer: A Monthly Magazine for Literary Workers,* Volume 15 (The Writer Publishing Company, 1902), p. 4. The entirety of the publication has been digitized by Google and is freely available at books.google.com.
3. Allyson J. Horgan, Melissa B. Russano, Christian A. Meissner, and Jacqueline R. Evans, "Minimization and Maximization Techniques: Assessing the Perceived Consequences of Confessing and Confession Diagnosticity," *Psychology, Crime & Law* (January 2011), *http://works.bepress.com/cgi/viewcontent.cgi?article=1055&context=christian_meissner*.
4. Ibid.

Chapter 10

1. Jodi Picoult, *Vanishing Acts* (Washington Square Press, 2005), p. 125.
2. Trevor Crow, e-mail to the author, August 4, 2014.
3. Kat McGowan, "Living a Lie," *Psychology Today,* January 2, 2013, *www.psychologytoday.com/articles/201212/living-lie*.
4. Joanna Starek, interviewed for "Deception" by Jad Abumrad and Robert Krulwich, Radiolab, Season 4, Episode 2, *www.radiolab.org/story/91612-deception/*.

5. Ruben Gur and Harold Sackeim, "Self-Deception: A Concept in Search of a Phenomenon," *Journal of Personality and Social Psychology* 37 (1979): 147–169, *http://bigfatgenius.com/3180/Self_Deception_Questionnaire.pdf.*

6. Joanna Starek, interviewed for "Deception" by Jad Abumrad and Robert Krulwich, Radiolab, Season 4, Episode 2, *www.radiolab.org/story/91612-deception/.*

7. Ibid.

8. Ibid.

9. Jean-Paul Sartre, *Being and Nothingness,* Reprint Edition (Washington Square Press, 1993).

Adaptors: Actions to release stress, as defined by body language expert Gregory Hartley

Advocacy journalism: News coverage that openly espouses a point of view

Agent: A person who volunteers or is recruited to provide information covertly to intelligence services

Analytic listening: Purposeful listening; a term created for this book

Asset: A person (*see* "Agent") or other resource supporting cover operations

Asset validation: The process used to vet a source

Barriers: Postures and objects that put separation between one person and another, as defined by body language expert Gregory Hartley

Cognitive Interview: Developed by Ronald P. Fisher and R. Edward Geiselman as a tool to help investigators improve their interviews with cooperative witnesses and victims

Compound question: A question that poses two or more questions at once; considered a bad question

Confabulation: A way of inadvertently conveying false information that has its roots in neurological disease

Control question: A question you know the answer to when you ask it

Cryptomnesia: Literally means "hidden memory"; refers to a phenomenon in which a person essentially steals from his or her own memory; a way of inadvertently conveying false information

Direct question: A straightforward question that opens with a basic interrogative

Dissembling phrase: A phrase designed to conceal the truth

Follow-up question: Also known as a persistent question; the same question either reshaped or repeated

HUMINT: Human intelligence

Illustrators: Movements that punctuate a statement, as defined by body language expert Gregory Hartley

Kinesics: An area of non-verbal communication that focuses on movement

Leading question: A question that supplies the answer; considered a bad question

Maximizing: A method to make your source feel more guilty than is warranted

Minimizing: A method to make your source feel less guilty than is warranted

Misattribution: The phenomenon of memory involving incorrect attribution; a way of inadvertently conveying false information

Negative question: A question relying on negative words with the result being confusing as to what is sought (a yes or a "no"); considered a bad question

Non-pertinent question: A question ostensibly unrelated to the information sought that may be used to get the source talking

Power pose: A standing or seated posture that conveys self-assuredness

Proxemics: An area of non-verbal communication that focuses on spatial relationships

Proximate reality: A phrase coined by Mark Lowenthal, former assistant director of Central Intelligence for Analysis & Product, to describe what intelligence professionals seek

REBLE: The acronym created by Lena Sisco to describe key skills she teaches through The Congruency Group: Relax, Establish rapport, Baseline, Look for deviations, and Extract the truth

Regulators: Movements used to regulate another person's speech, as defined by body language expert Gregory Hartley

Reliable facial muscles: A concept defined by psychologist Paul Ekman; he asserts that activation of these muscles communicates the presence of specific emotions

Repeat question: A question related to an earlier question that is seeking the same information

Shiin: The Japanese word to describe an awkward silence in a conversation

Somatic experience: A way of getting in touch with emotions and thoughts by focusing on body sensations

Sorting style: The way an individual sorts information (for example, in a sequential or random fashion)

Source amnesia: A memory phenomenon in which there is an inability to remember where knowledge came from; a way of inadvertently conveying false information

Summary question: A question allowing a source to revisit an
   answer

Vague question: A question that lacks clarity such that the
   source isn't sure what information is being requested;
   considered a bad question

Vocalics: An area of non-verbal communication studies
   focused on how words are spoken

In addition to my distinguished coauthors of previous human behavior books, **Gregory Hartley** (*How to Spot a Liar*) and **James O. Pyle** (*Find Out Anything From Anyone, Anytime*), the following intelligence professionals contributed meaningful content and essential background information to this book:

Elizabeth Bancroft serves as executive director of the Association of Former Intelligence Officers (AFIO). Previously, she was director of the National Intelligence Book Center, Washington, D.C., and served as managing editor of *Surveillant,* a bi-monthly intelligence publications review. A graduate of Harvard/Radcliffe, she is editor of AFIO's *Intelligencer* journal, as well as a computer specialist on text indexing/retrieval, bibliographic databases, and publishing. She served on the board of the National Intelligence Study Center and as vice president of the National Historical Intelligence Museum, and was an advisor to AFIO's board prior to being hired as management.

Ray Decker's career in military intelligence encompassed service in the European theater and, most recently, in Iraq and Afghanistan, where he held key liaison roles with the U.S. Marine Corps. He was responsible for the planning and execution of two national elections in Al Anbar province, Iraq (2005–2006), which were pivotal in supporting the establishment of a democratic government in Iraq. In Afghanistan, he was the 2nd Marine Expeditionary Brigades's senior operations liaison officer to the Italian-Spanish Combat Brigade in Herat (2009–2011). A graduate of the U.S. Naval Academy, he retired from the Marine Corps Reserve as a lieutenant colonel after 30 years of combined duty in operational and staff assignments stateside and abroad. His subsequent civilian career included serving as federal senior executive responsible for Combating Terrorism Assessments at the U.S. Government Accountability Office (GAO) before and after the attacks of September 11, 2001. His current role is managing director of ArgenRM, which advises clients on risk-influenced decision-making; collection and analysis of environmental intelligence; and strategic planning and operational execution.

Jack Devine is a 32-year veteran of the CIA, where he served as both acting director and associate director of the CIA's operations outside the United States. In this capacity, he had supervisory authority over thousands of CIA employees involved in sensitive missions throughout the world. He held numerous other senior positions at the CIA, such as chief of the Latin American Division and head of the Counternarcotics Center, which was responsible for coordinating and building close cooperation between all major U.S. and foreign law enforcement agencies in tracking worldwide narcotics and crime organizations in the 1980s. Devine also headed the CIA's Afghan Task Force, which successfully countered Soviet aggression in the region. He was awarded the CIA's Meritorious Officer Award for this accomplishment. Devine is the recipient of the Agency's Distinguished Intelligence Medal and several meritorious awards. He is a member of the Council on Foreign Relations, a board member of the CIA Memorial Foundation, and the author of *Good Hunting.* Devine is a founding partner and president of The Arkin Group, based in New York City.

E. Peter Earnest is executive director of the International Spy Museum and a 36-year veteran of the CIA, with a career that included more than 20 years in the Agency's Clandestine Service. A member of the CIA's Senior Intelligence Service, he was awarded the Agency's Intelligence Medal of Merit for superior performance throughout his career. He also served as the Agency's principal spokesman in his final posting, developing and implementing a strategy of greater openness with the media and the public. Earnest is coauthor with Maryann Karinch of *Business Confidential: Lessons for Corporate Success From Inside the CIA, Harry Potter and the Art of Spying* (coauthor Lynn Boughey), and *The Dictionary of Espionage* (coauthor Joseph Goulden).

Gary Harter has more than 30 years of experience with the FBI, with expertise in varied disciplines. Security stops in his post-bureau career include BearingPoint, where he served as a member of the IT Security Team. He assisted in investigations involving attempted intrusion incidents as well as integrity investigations, among other responsibilities. Upon leaving BearingPoint, Gary was hired by Computer Sciences Corporation (CSC) as a member of their security team. While at CSC, he assisted in forming the Dulles Area Information Sharing and Analysis Centers (ISAC), a local security organization. He currently serves as industry co-chair for the ISAC.

Oleg Danilovich Kalugin, KGB, is a retired major general in the 1st Chief Directorate of the KGB. General Kalugin was the youngest general in the history of the KGB. Early in his 32-year career, he worked undercover as a journalist while attending New York's Columbia University, and then conducted espionage and influence operations as a *Radio Moscow* correspondent with the United Nations. General Kalugin played a major role in the John Walker spy ring as deputy chief of the KGB station at the Soviet Embassy in Washington, D.C. He was also an elected member of the Soviet parliament during Gorbachev's administration and was one of the first reformers of the KGB. His book, *Spymaster: My Thirty-Two Years in Intelligence and Espionage Against the West,* chronicles his KGB career. He is currently a professor at The Centre for Counterintelligence and Security Studies in Alexandria, Virginia.

Eric B. Maddox is best known as the interrogator who conducted more than 300 interrogations and collected the intelligence that directly led to the capture of Saddam Hussein. He is a recipient of the National Intelligence Medal of Achievement, Defense Intelligence Agency (DIA) Director's Award, Legion of Merit, and Bronze Star, for his direct role in the capture of the former dictator. During 2004–2014, Maddox served in the federal government civil service, as an Intelligence Officer and Interrogator for the Department of Defense (DoD). He is the author of *Mission: Black List #1,* a factual and dramatic narrative about the hunt for Saddam Hussein. Maddox now serves as a security consultant for corporations, organizations, and individuals, in the areas of national security, interrogations/questioning, intelligence, site assessments, personal assessments, and extensive background investigation.

David G. Major is a retired FBI executive/supervisory special agent. During his 24-year FBI career specializing in all phases of counterintelligence, the first FBI official to be assigned as a staff officer on the National Security Council where he served as the director of Intelligence and Counterintelligence Programs during the Reagan administration. Major is founder and owner of the Centre for Counterintelligence and Security Studies (Cicentre.com) and president of DGMA, Inc. since 1997, teaching advance CI and CT courses for the U.S. national security community and private sector. He developed and manages SPYPEDIA®, the world's largest subscription database on espionage, terrorism, and cybersecurity, updated daily with CI/CT news and articles. Major serves as a founding and current member of the International Spy Museum's board of directors. He has 40-plus years as a counterintelligence practitioner and is a recognized leading authority and expert on counterintelligence/ security and counterterrorism. Major is a graduate of Syracuse University and served as a U.S. Army Captain.

Michael T. Reilly, whose military duties included special agent in the Coast Guard Investigative Service (CGIS), is currently deputy chief in the Fairfax, Virginia, County Office of the Fire Marshall. With a population exceeding one million, his jurisdiction is the most populous in both Virginia and the Washington, D.C. metropolitan area. Reilly's expertise in his current position is rooted in his work in hazardous materials, investigative services, fire prevention, and environmental crimes. He maintains a rank of chief warrant officer, United States Coast Guard Reserves. He is a member of the National Fire Protection Association, National Association of Fire Investigators, International Association of Arson Investigators, the State Fire Chief's Association of Virginia, International Association of Firefighters Local 2068, and the Fairfax County Fire Officers Association.

Lena Sisco is a former Department of Defense (DoD)–
certified military interrogator and naval officer who served
in the Global War on Terror. She is the recipient of the
Joint Service and the Navy/Marine Corp Commendation
and Achievement Medals. Sisco has extensive experience in
the field of human intelligence (HUMINT), has worked for
the Office of Naval Intelligence and Defense Intelligence
Agency, and partnered with the FBI and the Naval Criminal
Investigative Service in HUMINT Collection Activities. She
has been training DoD personnel in interrogation, tactical
questioning/debriefing, site exploitation, elicitation, counter-
elicitation, cross-cultural communications, HUMINT policy,
detecting deception, and behavioral congruency for more
than 10 years. In addition to instructing, Sisco has developed
courses and training curriculums and is Instructional Systems
Design certified. Sisco is certified as a Body Language Institute
Train-the-Trainer Instructor and instructs with Janine Driver.
In addition, she is Six Sigma certified. Prior to her career in
HUMINT, she received her master's degree in archaeology
from Brown University and excavated overseas. She founded
The Congruency Group in order to share her skills with DoD
and law enforcement personnel and the private sector in order
for individuals to achieve ultimate success in their personal
and professional endeavors, put criminals behind bars, and
gather intelligence information to save lives.

Maryann Karinch is the author of 21 books, most of which focus on human behavior. In recognition of her accomplishments in extreme sports and her work as a dedicated explorer of the psyche and mind-body interaction, The Explorers Club elected her to membership in 2010. She is also a member of The Authors Guild.

Maryann's most recent titles are *Find Out Anything From Anyone, Anytime* (Career Press, coauthor James Pyle), *Forging Healthy Connections* (New Horizon Press, coauthor Trevor Crow, LMFT), *The Wandering Mind* (Rowman & Littlefield, coauthor John Biever, MD), and *How to Spot a Liar* (Revised Edition, Career Press, coauthor Greg Hartley).

In 2004, Maryann founded The Rudy Agency, a literary agency specializing in non-fiction. Earlier in her career, she served as director of communications for a prominent lobbying organization. Before that, she managed a professional theater and raised funds for arts and education programs in Washington, D.C. She holds bachelor's and master's degrees in speech and drama from The Catholic University of America in Washington, D.C and is a Certified Personal Trainer (American Council on Exercise).

Her Website is *www.karinch.com*. She resides in Estes Park, Colorado.